CORRECT *your* ENGLISH ERRORS

Avoid 99% of the Common Mistakes Made by Learners of English

Tim Collins, Ph.D.

New York Chicago San Francisco Lisbon London Madrid Mexico City
Milan New Delhi San Juan Seoul Singapore Sydney Toronto

The McGraw·Hill Companies

Library of Congress Cataloging-in-Publication Data

Collins, Tim.
Correct your English errors : avoid 99% of the common mistakes made by learners of English / by Tim Collins.
p. cm.
Includes index.
ISBN 0-07-147050-6 (alk. paper)
1. English language—Textbooks for foreign speakers. 2. English language—Usage. 3. English language—Errors of usage. I. Title.

PE1128.C69385 2008
428.2'4—dc22 2008011218

12 13 14 15 16 17 18 19 20 21 DOC 21 20 19 18 17 16

ISBN 978-0-07-147050-6
MHID 0-07-147050-6

McGraw-Hill books are available at special quantity discounts to use as premiums and sales promotions or for use in corporate training programs. To contact a representative, please visit the Contact Us pages at www.mhprofessional.com.

This book is printed on acid-free paper.

CONTENTS

INTRODUCTION

The purpose of this book is to identify the most common trouble spots for English language learners, to provide a basis for understanding why these trouble spots cause difficulties, and to offer guidance and practice for avoiding potential errors.

Many errors commonly made by speakers and learners of a second language are caused by transferring patterns and features of the native language to the new language. This happens in all aspects of language from pronunciation to word formation to sentence structure:

- Difficulty saying an English sound arises because the first language does not have such a sound.
- Double letters are omitted from English words because the first language's spelling system does not have double letters.
- Verb endings to show tense or noun endings to show plurals are omitted because the first language does not add such suffixes to these words.
- Adjectives are placed after, rather than before, nouns because the first language follows that pattern.
- "Taller from" is said instead of "taller than" because that's the pattern in the first language.

Another source of error is the learning process itself. That is, learners tend to overapply or misapply patterns and rules in the new language, do not learn exceptions to the rules, or do not apply the rules fully. Here are examples of these kinds of errors:

- Applying the regular *-ed* past-tense ending to irregular verbs: *I goed home early yesterday.*
- Using *more* with the adjective *heavy* (which requires the *-er* ending) because the rule that two-syllable adjectives ending in *-y* use *-er*, not *more*, was not fully learned.
- Using *asleep* in front of a noun because the rule that a certain small group of adjectives, including *asleep*, are used only after a linking verb was not fully learned.

In this book, you will find help with these and many more common errors through explanation and example. You will become aware of potential trouble spots and learn how to break the habits, learn the necessary rules, and correct your mistakes. Several examples are given for each topic, followed by exercises that test your understanding and help you avoid the pitfalls.

Because individual words of a language are used in connection with other words, you will find that many topics are mentioned in more than one place. Extensive cross-referencing will help you find connections between related topics. Topics and lists are presented in logical order. For example, irregular verbs are presented in groups of verbs that follow similar patterns. Comparative and superlative forms of adjectives are presented in logical groupings according to how they are formed and spelled. Verb tenses are presented in order from the present tense to modal verbs. Complex syntactic patterns, such as the passive voice, are presented at the end of the volume, after all the prerequisite knowledge has been presented. In addition, the back of the book includes a comprehensive and detailed index, which serves as a guide to locating all the references to each topic, as well as a key with the answers to all the exercises. I hope that the materials presented in this book will help you improve your proficiency in English and avoid the most common and vexing errors in English.

Suggestions for Using this Book

This book is divided into two parts: Pronunciation and Spelling and Grammar. The largest section is Grammar, which identifies the various parts of speech in traditional terminology for ease of comprehension. Each term is explained and illustrated with multiple examples, providing necessary review or clarification.

There are many ways to use this book:

- Examine the "Avoid the Error" headings in each section. Read the examples and then the related explanations.
- Use the index to find specific topics, as you need them.
- Use the table of contents to find the specific chapters you want to study.
- Work through the book in sequence from beginning to end for a complete overview or review of English grammar and the most common and vexing errors that learners make.
- Complete the exercises on your own paper, and use the Answer Key to check your work. Then review any areas where you need extra review or explanation, and complete the exercises again.

- Use the "Catch the Errors" section at the end of the book to check your understanding of the major topics in the book.

Throughout this book, all errors are presented in red type and marked by an ✘. For maximum clarity, all errors are corrected, and each corrected version is presented with a ✔.

The guidelines here are based on current standard usage in North America. However, usage varies according to region and other variables, and language is constantly changing. In cases where variants exist for formal and informal situations, details are provided. The biggest error of all would be to correct a native speaker, or to imply in any way that he or she does not speak correct English. The best way to improve your English is to listen to native speakers and interact with them.

ACKNOWLEDGMENTS

I am indebted to Grace Freedson, who presented me with the opportunity to write this book; to Garret Lemoi, who gave patient guidance and feedback throughout the writing; to Julia Anderson Bauer, who skillfully put the book through the publishing process; to Robert F. Wilson, whose networking skills have been instrumental in my career; and to Mary Jane Maples, who has provided me with peerless advice and countless opportunities throughout my career.

This book is dedicated to all my teachers of linguistics:

Cynthia Cornell, DePauw University
Ernesto Carratalá, Universitat Central de Barcelona
Roser Estapá Argemí, Universitat Central de Barcelona
José Enrique Gargallo Gil, Universitat Central de Barcelona
Joan Veny, Universitat Central de Barcelona
Lyle Bachman, University of California at Los Angeles
Mario Saltarelli, University of Southern California
H. Douglas Brown, San Francisco State University
Lawrence F. Bouton, University of Illinois at Urbana
Ron Cowan, University of Illinois at Urbana
Wayne B. Dickerson, University of Illinois at Urbana
Pearl Goodman, University of Illinois at Urbana
Hans Hock, University of Illinois at Urbana
Yamuna Kachru, University of Illinois at Urbana
James F. Lee, Indiana University
Bill VanPatten, University of Illinois at Chicago
Carol Klee, University of Minnesota
John Bordie, University of Texas at Austin
Jabier Elorrieta, University of Texas at Austin
Elaine Horwitz, University of Texas at Austin
Zena Moore, University of Texas at Austin
Dieter Wanner, The Ohio State University

PRONUNCIATION AND SPELLING

PRONUNCIATION

English Sounds

The English language has about forty sounds, twenty-four consonants, and sixteen vowels. Knowing these sounds can help you improve your pronunciation. Special phonetic symbols are used to represent sounds. Key places in this book use phonetic symbols to clarify pronunciation. They are written between slash marks, such as /b/, to indicate that they are symbols. You do not need to memorize these symbols to learn English—just use them as references. Many learners' dictionaries use these symbols, so being familiar with them will help you when you look up words. Each of these sounds can be spelled in many ways. For information on spelling, see page 9.

Consonants

This table shows the consonant sounds of English:

VOICELESS

/p/	**p**o**p**, **p**u**pp**y
/t/	**t**ime, ho**t**el, ho**t**
/k/	**k**ill, Mi**k**e
/f/	**f**ind, lea**f**
/s/	**s**eat, in**s**ect, ba**ss**
/ʃ/	**sh**eep, **sh**ip, fini**sh**
/tʃ/	**ch**ur**ch**
/θ/	**th**ink, ei**th**er, fai**th**
/h/	**h**appy

VOICED

/b/	**b**oy, **b**a**bb**le, **b**la**b**
/d/	**d**one, **d**a**d**
/g/	**g**et, sa**gg**ing, hu**g**
/v/	**v**olume, lea**v**es, o**f**
/z/	**z**ebra, bu**zz**ard, a**s**
/ʒ/	a**z**ure, vi**s**ion

/dʒ/	**j**u**dg**e
/ð/	**th**ough, al**th**ough
/l/	**l**ong, fo**ll**ow, **l**u**ll**
/m/	**m**uch, su**mm**er, co**m**e
/n/	**N**ancy, su**nn**y, moo**n**
/ŋ/	ri**ng**, si**ng**
/r/	**r**est, **r**ea**r**
/w/	**w**o**w**, q**u**een
/y/	**y**es, be**y**ond, **E**urope

Voiced and Voiceless Sounds

Consonants fall into two groups, voiced and voiceless. When you say a voiced sound, your vocal chords vibrate. When you say a voiceless sound, your vocal chords do not vibrate. To feel your vocal chords vibrate, place your hand on your throat and say word pairs such as *fan/van*, *pill/bill*, or *Sue/zoo*. Your vocal chords should not vibrate when you say the first consonant in each pair.

Many learners have difficulty with the sounds /θ/ and /ð/. The sound /θ/ is not voiced (i.e., it is voiceless), which means the vocal chords do not vibrate when you say it. The sound /ð/ is voiced. The chords should vibrate when you say this consonant.

AVOID THE Error

To pronounce /θ/ and /ð/, your tongue must be between the upper and lower teeth. Instead, people may make the mistake of saying /d/ or another sound.

✗ dis ✓ this

The sounds /θ/ and /ð/ may be difficult for individuals from a culture where it is not polite to show your tongue. Keep in mind that when speaking English, showing one's tongue to pronounce these sounds is perfectly normal. Nevertheless, if you are shy, you might cover your mouth when you say these sounds, until you become comfortable saying them.

To learn /r/, listen to native speakers and practice saying words with many /r/ sounds, such as *refrigerator.* Saying tongue twisters is also a good way to practice this sound.

Around the rough rocks the angry rascal ran.

AVOID THE Error

The sounds /l/ and /r/ are often difficult for speakers of Chinese, Japanese, Korean, and other Asian languages. In fact, their listeners can become confused by the wrong sound:

right	✘ /l/ light	✔ /r/ right
lock	✘ /r/ rock	✔ /l/ lock
grass	✘ /l/ glass	✔ /r/ grass

Word pairs that can be confused in this way include: *right/light, lock/rock, grass/glass, lamp/ramp, raw/law, row/low.*

The sound /l/ is produced by the tip of the tongue touching the roof of the mouth. The sound /r/ involves no contact between the tongue and the roof of the mouth.

The spelling of words in English is a reliable clue for when to pronounce each sound. The letter *l* is always pronounced /l/, and the letter *r* is always pronounced /r/. However, some words have a silent *l*: *would, could, should, half, chalk, talk, walk, Lincoln, almond,* and *salmon.*

Vowels

This table shows the vowel sounds of English:

/i/	eat, meet, sea, need	/ɪ/	bit, hit, him, sit
/e/	bait, name	/ɛ/	bet, bed, peck
/aɪ/	fine, bite, kite, might	/a/	not, bottle, father, hot
/o/	boat, go, show	/æ/	bat, cat, black
/u/	boot, food, shoe	/ʊ/	book, put
/ɔy/	boy, toy		
/ɔ/	bought, coffee, dog		
/aʊ/	house		
/ʌ/	but, none, sun, cup *(stressed syllables only)*		
/ə/	about, focus, cinema *(unstressed syllables only)*		
/ɛr/	bird		

The /ɛr/ sound is particularly hard to say. To learn it, practice saying words with vowel + r combinations.

bird third heard absurd

Stress

Stress is the loudness with which we say a word or syllable. (A syllable is a part of a word that consists of at least one vowel and can have one or more consonants. A word can consist of one or more syllables.) A word can have one or more stressed syllables. A one- or two-syllable word can have one stressed syllable.

'din ner 'sci ence 'food

A word of two or more syllables can have primary stress and secondary stress. Primary stress is marked with ', secondary stress with ˌ.

ˌmath e 'ma tics ˌun der 'stand ing

Some words, such as articles and one-syllable prepositions, are not stressed at all.

of a an in on

In English, unstressed vowels usually become /ə/.

of /əv/ the /thə/ but /bət/

AVOID THE *Error*

Sometimes the meaning of a word depends on which syllable is stressed.

✗ He is a main sus**pect**.	✓ He is the main **sus**pect.
✗ The police **sus**pect he is the criminal.	✓ The police sus**pect** he is the criminal.

In ***suspect/suspect*** and many other pairs of words, the first syllable is stressed if the word is a noun, but the second syllable is stressed if the word is a verb.

	FIRST SYLLABLE STRESSED	SECOND SYLLABLE STRESSED
addict	a person who is addicted to drugs (noun)	to be addicted to drugs (verb)
defect	a shortcoming in a product (noun)	to give up your citizenship (verb)
convert	a person who changes religions (noun)	to change into another, as in changing religion (verb)
suspect	a person you suspect (noun)	to suspect someone (verb)
conflict	a disagreement or clash (noun)	to disagree or clash (verb)
record	a record of something (noun)	to record information (verb)

Contrastive Stress

In English, we can stress any word, even one that normally is not stressed, to express a special meaning. Look at how the meaning of this sentence changes depending on the stress:

We will finish work at 1:00. (Others will finish at another time.)
We **will** finish work at 1:00. (We won't finish at another time.)
We will **finish** work at 1:00. (We won't start or do something else at that time.)
We will finish **work** at 1:00. (We won't work after that time.)
We will finish work **at** 1:00. (We will finish at exactly that time.)
We will finish work at **1:00**. (We will not finish at 2:00.)

Listen carefully when English speakers give special stress to a certain word. It means that the person is using contrastive stress.

Rising Intonation for Questions

Intonation is the pitch, higher or lower, of sound. English uses rising intonation for *yes/no* questions. With rising intonation, the pitch goes up at the end of the sentence. The rising intonation signals that the person is asking a question.

Are you finished using the computer?

AVOID THE *Error*

Do not use rising intonation with *wh-* questions. Use falling intonation.

✘ When does the movie begin? (rising intonation)

✔ When does the movie begin? (falling intonation)

In *wh-* questions, the question word signals that the person is asking a question. Rising intonation is not necessary with *wh-* questions.

SPELLING

English spelling often seems difficult, but many common spelling patterns can help us spell better.

Vowels

Short Vowels

Spell short vowels /ɪ, ɛ, æ, ɔ, ʊ/ with only one letter.

red it pot pen mad

Long Vowels

To spell long vowels /i, e, o, u/, use two letters.

SHORT	LONG
mat	mat**e**
rid	rid**e**
mad	ma**i**d

Usually, the second vowel is silent. To remember this rule, children use a simple rhyme. You can use it, too: "When two vowels go walking, the first one does the talking."

A vowel that comes at the end of a word or syllable also is long.

po**n**y mu**s**ic

i Before *e*

When the letters *i* and *e* are together, they are usually spelled *ie*.

rel**ie**f fr**ie**nd bel**ie**ve v**ie**w

There are some exceptions to this rule:

- After *c*, *e* usually comes before *i*.

  dec**ei**ve receiv**ei**ve

- When the combination sounds like /a/, *e* comes before *i*.

  n**ei**ghbor w**ei**gh w**ei**ght fr**ei**ght **ei**ght

However, not all words follow this pattern:

w**ei**rd for**ei**gn l**ei**sure

A children's rhyme makes this rule memorable: "*I* before *e,* except after *c* or when sounded as /a/, as in *neighbor* and *weigh*."

Consonants

The sound /f/ can be spelled with *f*, *ph-*, *-ough*, or *-augh*.

find	**ph**one	en**ough**	la**ugh**
e**ff**ort	**ph**oto	r**ough**	la**ugh**ter
gol**f**	al**ph**abet	t**ough**	la**ugh**ed
che**f**	gra**ph**	c**ough**	

There are some exceptions to these rules. The letter group *-ough* also represents /o/.

b**ough** d**ough**

The letter group *-augh* represents the sounds /ɔ/.

d**augh**ter c**augh**t h**augh**ty

AVOID THE Error

The initial /f/ sound in *Philippines* (an island nation in Asia) is spelled *Ph-*, but *Filipino* (an individual from that country) is spelled with *F*.

✘ Filippines	✔ Philippines
✘ Philipino	✔ Filipino

The sound /k/ can be spelled *c*, *cc*, *k*, or *ck*.

ba**ck** **c**a**k**e o**cc**ur

The letter *q* is always followed by *u*.

quick	quiet	quit	question
quality	qualification	quiz	

The /s/ sound can be spelled with *c* or *s*. Usually *c* + *i* or *e* is pronounced /s/. Otherwise, *c* is usually pronounced /k/.

/s/	said	usually	cede	excellent	cider
/k/	company	computer	cucumber	calculate	

The /ʤ/ sound can be spelled with *g* or *j*. Usually, *g* + *i* or *e* is pronounced /ʤ/. Otherwise, *g* is usually pronounced /g/.

/ʤ/	judge	Jones	joke	jack	gel	genuine	giant
/g/	go	golf	gum	grumpy	glum	gap	

AVOID THE Error

Don't forget the double consonant letters in English words.

✘ leter	✔ letter
✘ ful	✔ full
✘ litle	✔ little
✘ suces	✔ success

Silent Letters

Many words have silent letters.

- The *k* is silent in the initial *kn-*.

  knight knife knee know knowledge

- The letters *gh* are silent in the final *-ght*.

  height eight flight light might right

- The letter *b* is silent before *t* in words such as:

  debt doubt

- The letters *h* and *w* are silent in these combinations: *rh-* and *wr-*.

rhyme	wrestle	wrong
rhythm	write	
rhino	wrap	

- An initial *h* is silent in many words.

honor **herb** **hour** **heir**

- The letter *l* is silent in these words:

should **could** **would**

- Many words end with a silent final *-e*.

rake **take** **make** **stake** **brake**

AVOID THE *Error*

Take care not to forget a final silent *-e*.

✗ lik	✓ like
✗ bik	✓ bike

Adding Prefixes

A prefix is a word part added to the beginning of a word to change its meaning. Common prefixes include *mis-*, *over-*, *pre-*, and *re-*. Adding a prefix to a word does not change the spelling of the word.

AVOID THE *Error*

If the last letter of a prefix and the first letter of a word are the same, the letter will appear double when the prefix and word are combined. Do not forget the double letter.

mis + state	✗ mistate	✓ mis**s**tate
un + necessary	✗ unecessary	✓ un**n**ecessary
mis + spell	✗ mispell	✓ mis**s**pell
pre + eminent	✗ preminent	✓ pre**e**minent

Adding Suffixes

Suffixes are word parts that are added to the ends of words. Common suffixes include *-ed*, *-ing*, *-er*, *est*, *-s*, *-ful*, *-ly*, and so on. Adding suffixes to words involves many spelling changes. Here are some simple rules.

When adding a suffix that ends in a vowel to a one-syllable word that ends in a vowel and a single consonant *(hot)*, double the final consonant: *hotter.*

hot + -er	hotter	**big** + -est	biggest
hit + -ing	hitting	**stop** + -ed	stopped

This is often called the **1 + 1 + 1 rule**. If a word has a one-syllable word, one short vowel, and one consonant at the end, then double the consonant when adding a suffix.

If a word has more than one syllable, double the final consonant only if the final syllable is stressed.

FIRST SYLLABLE IS STRESSED		FINAL SYLLABLE IS STRESSED	
travel + **er**	traveler	begin + **ing**	beginning
open + **ed**	opened		

When adding a suffix to a word that ends in consonant + *-y*, change the final *-y* to *-i*.

cry + ed	cried	fry + es	fries
lady + s	ladies		

When adding a suffix to a word that ends in a vowel + *-y*, do not change the final *-y* to *-i*.

stay + -ed	stayed	**play** + -ful	playful
stay + -s	stays		

When adding a suffix to a word that ends in a vowel, drop the final vowel if the suffix begins with a vowel.

nice + -est	nicest	bore + -ed	bored
make + -ing	making		

AVOID THE Error

Do not drop the final *-e* when it comes before *c* or *g* and the suffix begins in *a*, *o*, or *u*.

manage + -able	✗ managable	✔ manageable
courage + -ous	✗ couragous	✔ courageous
notice + -able	✗ noticable	✔ noticeable

When adding *-able* to *like* or *love*, dropping the *-e* is optional:

lik**e**able	lov**e**able
likable	lovable

When adding a suffix to a word that ends in a vowel, keep the final vowel if the suffix begins with a consonant.

love + -ly	lov**e**ly

For details on adding

- *-s* to nouns, see page 47.
- *-s* to verbs, see page 131.
- *-ing* to verbs, see page 138.
- *-ed* to verbs, see page 150.
- *-er/-est* to adjectives, see page 105.
- *-ly* to adjectives, see page 223.
- *-er/-est* to adverbs, see page 233.

Contractions

Contractions are short forms for two words written together. Use an apostrophe to spell a contraction. The apostrophe replaces the letters that have been deleted from the contraction.

do + not	don**'t**	will + not	won**'t**	does + not	doesn**'t**
he + is	he**'s**	they + are	they**'re**	he + had	he**'d**

AVOID THE *Error*

Don't confuse the common contractions *they're*, *it's*, and *you're* with other words:

- ***They're* is the contraction of *they are*.** Writers often confuse *they're* with the possessive adjective *their* or the adverb *there*.

✗ **There** busy today. ✓ **They're** busy today.

✗ **Their** busy today.

- ***It's* is the contraction of *it is*.** Writers often confuse *it's* with the possessive adjective *its*.

✗ **Its** sunny today. ✓ **It's** sunny today.

- ***You're* is the contraction of *you are*.** Writers often confuse *you're* with the possessive adjective *your*.

✗ **Your** at work so early today, Margaret. ✓ **You're** at work so early today, Margaret.

Compound Words

Compound words are two words that come together to form a new word. Compound words can be spelled as single words, with hyphens, or as two separate words.

news + paper	newspaper	butter + fly	butterfly
second + hand	secondhand		
six + pack	six-pack	mass + produced	mass-produced
son + in + law	son-in-law		
post + office	post office	real + estate	real estate
park + bench	park bench		

AVOID THE *Error*

Thank you is written as two words.

✘ **Thankyou** for your support. ✔ **Thank you** for your support.

When compound words are pronounced, the first word is always stressed.

mailbox **post** office **postage** stamp **post**mark

To spell a compound word, say the parts aloud. If the first word is not stressed, it's not a compound. Spell it as two words without a hyphen. If the first word is stressed, then the entire word is a compound. Check a dictionary to see if a space or a hyphen is needed.

Homonyms

Homonyms are words that sound the same but have different spellings and meanings. Using an incorrect homonym is very confusing to readers. The following table shows some common homonyms:

accept	except
ad	add
affect	effect
be	bee
bear	bare
by	buy
fair	fare
here	hear
hour	our

in	inn	
its	it's	
know	no	
meet	meat	
principal	principle	
right	write	
there	their	they're
to too	two	
weather	whether	
who's	whose	
whole	hole	
you're	your	

AVOID THE *Error*

Be careful to use the correct homonym. Using the wrong homonym is very confusing to readers.

✘ Our car wouldn't start. It needed a **toe**.	✔ Our car wouldn't start. It needed a **tow**.
✘ That car should **break** down.	✔ That car should **brake** down.
✘ Phyllis is my favorite **ant**.	✔ Phyllis is my favorite **aunt**.
✘ The wind **blue** down several trees.	✔ The wind **blew** down several trees.
✘ I love you, **deer**.	✔ I love you, **dear**.
✘ The **facts** machine is not working.	✔ The **fax** machine is not working.
✘ He **nose**.	✔ He **knows**.
✘ The team **one** the game.	✔ The team **won** the game.
✘ She cooked a **stake** for dinner.	✔ She cooked a **steak** for dinner.
✘ We saw a **bare** in the woods.	✔ We saw a **bear** in the woods.
✘ **Hour** clock is fast.	✔ **Our** clock is fast.

If you type on a computer, the spell-checker can help you catch many spelling errors. However, it will not always catch errors when you type one homonym instead of another.

Give me a **stake**. Give me a **steak**.

Make sure you use the word you really mean.

AVOID THE Error

Some common spelling errors are the result of quick or careless keyboarding. Instead of typing one word, such as *or*, we type a similar word by mistake, such as *of*.

✗ Do you want cake **of** pie?	✓ Do you want cake **or** pie?
✗ This pie is made **or** fresh pumpkin.	✓ This pie is made **of** fresh pumpkin.

Watch for errors such as:

✗ form	✓ from	✗ from	✓ form
✗ of	✓ or	✗ or	✓ of
✗ read	✓ red	✗ red	✓ read
✗ then	✓ than	✗ than	✓ then
✗ loose	✓ lose	✗ lose	✓ loose

Good spelling takes careful proofreading. Ideally, you should check your writing for errors several times. Always double-check your writing for correct spelling.

AVOID THE *Error*

Avoid these common spelling errors when you proofread.

✘ adres, addres, adress	✔ address
✘ alot	✔ a lot
✘ alright	✔ all right
✘ can not	✔ cannot
✘ carear	✔ career
✘ Febuary	✔ February
✘ libary	✔ library
✘ licence	✔ license
✘ mispell	✔ misspell
✘ ninty	✔ ninety
✘ potatoe	✔ potato
✘ preceed	✔ precede
✘ sanwich, sanwitch, sandwitch	✔ sandwich
✘ suprise	✔ surprise
✘ thier	✔ their
✘ vacume	✔ vacuum
✘ Wensday	✔ Wednesday
✘ writting	✔ writing

Internet Spellings

The Internet has resulted in the creation of many new words and spelling problems. Because the Internet is so new and new ideas emerge so quickly, many terms have several spellings. Here are some common Internet terms:

Internet
e-mail *or* email
web site *or* Web site
online

URL
blog
LISTSERV

Check with your teacher, coworker, or boss about exactly how you should spell these terms if you need to use them.

AVOID THE *Error*

People use many abbreviations on the Internet. These abbreviations are fine for informal communication online, but not for work or school settings. Use the full forms for work and school.

✗ @	✓ at
✗ How RU?	✓ How are you?
✗ I 8 dinner.	✓ I ate dinner.
✗ K8 is a friend of mine.	✓ Kate is a friend of mine.

Do not spell out @ in e-mail addresses.

✓ TCollins@nl.edu

Of course, English has many more rules and each rule has exceptions. To help you improve your spelling, keep a spelling notebook. Note the spellings of words that you need to use often. You will be surprised how quickly your spelling improves.

Exercises

A *Spell the words correctly.*

1. adres ____________________
2. can not ____________________
3. thier ____________________
4. mispel ____________________
5. vacume ____________________
6. writting ____________________
7. libarry ____________________
8. milc ____________________

9. foriegn ___________________
10. alot ___________________

B *Complete the sentences by circling the correct word.*

1. The zoo has several brown and black (**bares/bears**).
2. Excuse me. I need to blow my (**nose/knows**).
3. (**Whose/Who's**) going to go on the field trip tomorrow?
4. (**It's/Its**) time for lunch.
5. (**Aunts/Ants**) can make a picnic lunch in the park unpleasant.
6. I think that Victor and April forgot (**they're/their/there**) umbrella.
7. We will leave in an (**hour/our**).
8. Did the waiter (**add/ad**) the bill correctly?
9. This tea is too (**suite/sweet**)! How much sugar is in it?
10. With sales (**tacks/tax**), your total is $93.47.

C *Find the misspelled word. Write it correctly.*

1. Please complete this from and return it to us. ___________________
2. Thankyou for helping me yesterday. ___________________
3. I red about that in the newspaper yesterday. ___________________
4. I am happy to meat you, Mrs. Williams. ___________________
5. I need to right an e-mail to my sister this afternoon. ___________________
6. Tom is taller then his little brother. ___________________
7. Please buy a sixpack of soda when you are at the store. ___________________
8. Andy does'nt like to eat meat. ___________________
9. Yesterday, the store openned at 9 A.M., but today is Sunday, so it won't open until 11 A.M. ___________________
10. His spelling is so bad that he could mispell his own name. ___________________

CAPITALIZATION

English has a number of rules for capitalization. In English you should capitalize:

- **The first letter of the first word of a sentence.** Always capitalize the first letter of the first word of a sentence.

  His phone rang several times during the meeting.
  Everyone should eat more vegetables.

- **The pronoun I.** Always capitalize the pronoun *I.*

  In general, **I** try to get to work early.
  I always pay my bills on time.

- **Proper nouns.** Proper nouns refer to a specific person, place, event, or group. Always capitalize proper nouns.

  Anne and Irene just got new jobs. (*Anne* and *Irene* are the names of two people.)
  Let's go swimming at Lake Park. (*Lake Park* is the name of a specific place.)
  Many children in our neighborhood are in the Boy Scouts. (*Boy Scouts* is the name of a specific group.)
  In 2008, the Olympics were in China. (*Olympics* is the name of a specific event.)

AVOID THE *Error*

Capitalize words such as *bank*, *church*, *library*, and so on only when they name a specific place.

✗ I need to go to the Bank.	✓ I need to go to North Community Bank.
✗ She goes to Church regularly.	✓ She goes to Parkville Community Church regularly.

Company names are proper nouns.

He works for **D**uke **P**ower **C**ompany.

I believe that **M**icrosoft **C**orporation is one of the most successful companies in the world.

AVOID THE *Error*

Capitalize brand names.

✗ Do you want a **coke?**	✓ Do you want a **Coke?**
✗ Please buy me a **hershey** bar.	✓ Please buy me a **Hershey** bar.

To avoid using brand names, use another word.

Do you want a **soda?**

Please buy me a **chocolate** bar.

In a few cases, a brand name has become the main way people refer to certain products. With these words, some people may find the equivalents unclear.

Kleenex (tissue)

Band-Aid (bandage)

Capitalize names of religions and words that come from them.

Islam	Christianity	Buddhism	Taoism	Judaism
Muslim	Christian	Buddhist	Taoist	Jew

Capitalize religious festivals.

Christmas Diwali Passover Ramadan

AVOID THE *Error*

Do not capitalize the names of religious rites, ceremonies, or activities.

✗ The **F**uneral is at 2:00.	✓ The **f**uneral is at 2:00.
✗ Let's say a few words of **P**rayer together, shall we?	✓ Let's say a few words of **p**rayer together, shall we?

These words follow this rule:

baptism prayer worship wedding funeral

Capitalize *God* when it refers to the deity.

Most Christian religious groups worship **G**od on Sundays.

AVOID THE *Error*

Do not capitalize *god* if that god is no longer worshipped.

✘ Zeus was the chief Greek **G**od.

✔ Zeus was the chief Greek **g**od.

Capitalize special events.

January is **A**frican **A**merican **H**istory **M**onth.

Capitalize holidays.

I am going camping over **L**abor **D**ay weekend.
Our town always has a parade on **M**emorial **D**ay.

AVOID THE *Error*

The United States has a number of special days to recognize people's and group's special interests. These days are capitalized, but are not considered actual holidays.

✘ **N**ational **p**ig **d**ay is March 1 of each year.

✔ **N**ational **P**ig **D**ay is March 1 of each year.

✘ January is **f**rozen **f**ood **m**onth.

✔ January is **F**rozen **F**ood **M**onth.

Internet is considered a proper noun.

Elizabeth met her latest boyfriend on the **I**nternet.

AVOID THE *Error*

Do not capitalize terms such as *e-mail*.

✘ I get too much **E**-mail.

✔ I get too much **e**-mail.

Proper Adjectives

Proper adjectives are adjectives that are formed from proper nouns. Always capitalize proper adjectives. Here are some proper adjectives and the proper nouns they come from.

PROPER NOUN	PROPER ADJECTIVE
America	American
France	French
Shakespeare	Shakespearean

Let's buy some **F**rench bread to have with dinner.
He read a beautiful **S**hakespearean poem.

Some people do not capitalize *French* when it's a part of a compound word, such as *French fries*. They write *french fries*.

I want some French fries, please.
I want some french fries, please.

Nouns Formed from Proper Nouns

Some nouns are formed from proper nouns. These words are often related to places. Always capitalize nouns formed from proper nouns.

Chicago	Chicagoan
Texas	Texan

Many **C**hicagoans enjoy its annual food festival, Taste of Chicago.

People's Titles

Capitalize people's titles when they are used with a name. People's titles include *Mr.*, *Mrs.*, *Miss*, *Ms.*, *Professor*, and *Dr.*

Let's ask **P**rofessor Ragan our question.
Right now Sam is getting a checkup at **D**r. Chow's office.

Do not confuse *Mrs.*, *Miss*, and *Ms.* Use *Mrs.* for married women and *Miss* for single women.

Miss Tate is getting married next week. Soon she'll be **Mrs.** Schwartzenbach.

AVOID THE *Error*

When writing *Miss*, do not use a period.

✘ **Miss.** Appleby was my best teacher in elementary school.

✔ **Miss** Appleby was my best teacher in elementary school.

Use *Ms.* for either single or married women. If you do not know whether a woman is single or married, use *Ms.* This title is useful in business settings.

Ms. North is in charge of telephone sales at this company.

AVOID THE *Error*

Do not capitalize a title when it is used without a name.

✘ He needs to see a **D**octor about that cough.

✔ He needs to see a **d**octor about that cough.

✘ I hate going to the **D**entist.

✔ I hate going to the **d**entist.

✘ That **P**rofessor's classes are very difficult.

✔ That **p**rofessor's classes are very difficult.

Always capitalize the title *President* when it refers to the U.S. President, whether it's used with or without a name.

The **President** gave a speech on TV last night.
President Kennedy was the greatest **President** in recent history.

AVOID THE *Error*

Do not capitalize the word *president* when it refers to the president of a company and is used without a name.

✘ All expenses greater than $10,000 must be approved by the **P**resident of the company.

✔ All expenses greater than $10,000 must be approved by the **p**resident of the company.

Capitalize job titles when they are at the end of a letter.

Sincerely,	Yours truly,
Frank Sloan	Mary Pierce
Senior **V**ice-**P**resident	**P**resident

Titles of Books, Movies, and TV Shows

Capitalize the first word, last word, and the important words (nouns, verbs, adjectives, and adverbs) of the titles of books, articles, plays, TV shows, songs, and movies. Do not capitalize unimportant words, such as articles (*a*, *the*) or prepositions (*in*, *on*), unless they are the first or last word in the title.

Her favorite TV show is "**F**riends."
"**D**ust in the **W**ind" (a song)
Love Story (a movie)

If a word such as a preposition or article is the first, last, or main word in a title, then capitalize it.

Ms. Phillip's favorite soap opera is "**T**he **Y**oung and the **R**estless."
My favorite book is ***Of Mice and Men***.
"**U**p, **U**p, and **A**way!" (a song)

AVOID THE *Error*

In a title, if a preposition is part of a two-word verb, then capitalize it.

✗ "Get **u**p, Stand **u**p" ✓ "Get **U**p, Stand **U**p"

For information on two-word verbs, see page 200.

Days of the Week and Months of the Year

Capitalize days of the week and months of the year.

Your appointment is on **T**hursday, **J**uly 5, at 5:00.
My birthday is **J**uly 15.

AVOID THE *Error*

Do not capitalize seasons.

✘ My favorite season is **S**pring. ✔ My favorite season is **s**pring.

✘ I need a **W**inter jacket. ✔ I need a **w**inter jacket.

School Subjects

Capitalize names of classes at school.

I am taking U.S. **H**istory this year.
I really like **A**dvanced **B**iology.

AVOID THE *Error*

Do not capitalize subjects in school unless they are the title of a specific class.

✘ Marta's favorite subject is **M**ath. ✔ Marta's favorite subject is **m**ath.

✘ She is taking **a**dvanced **m**ath 3 this year. ✔ She is taking **A**dvanced **M**ath 3 this year.

Always capitalize *U.S.*, *American*, and *English*, whether they refer to a class, a school subject, a language, or a country.

- I am taking **E**nglish Grammar 2 this year.
- I am good at **E**nglish.

Geography

Capitalize geographic regions of countries.

The **N**orth and the **S**outh fought a civil war beginning in 1860.
Illinois, Iowa, and Indiana are all in the **M**idwest.

AVOID THE Error

Do not capitalize *north*, *south*, *east*, or *west* when they do not refer to a part of the country.

✗ I live on the **N**orth side of town.

✓ I live on the **n**orth side of town.

✗ The **n**orth won the U.S. Civil War.

✓ The **N**orth won the U.S. Civil War.

Exercises

A *Rewrite the names and titles, using correct capital letters.*

1. *indiana jones and the temple of doom*

   ____

2. dr. william a. white

   ____

3. miss mary applebee

   ____

4. *on the waterfront*

   ____

5. sinclair county public schools

   ____

6. burbleson air force base

   ____

7. advanced biology

   ____

8. *victory on the high seas*

   ____

9. *harry potter and the order of the phoenix*

____

10. president john f. kennedy

____

B *Rewrite the sentences, using correct capital letters.*

1. John and i went to century Park for a Picnic Lunch.

____

2. Your next appointment with the Doctor is Tuesday, july 26, at 11:30 In the Morning.

____

3. Next Summer we want to go on Vacation in texas.

____

4. Let's go to the Movies. We can see *Detectives and robbers*.

____

5. "I love lucy" is a famous TV show starring Lucille ball.

____

6. In the Fall, I am going to take English grammar 2.

____

7. I like reading Books about American History.

____

8. My state's Senator is running for president.

____

PUNCTUATION

We use punctuation to make the meaning of words and sentences clear. The most important punctuation marks are the period, comma, question mark, exclamation mark, colon, semicolon, and quotation marks.

period	.
comma	,
question mark	?
exclamation mark	!
colon	:
semicolon	;
quotation marks	“ ”

Period

Use a period in these situations:

- **At the end of a sentence.** Use a period to end a sentence that is not an exclamation or a question.

My car needs new tires.
Rhonda is an excellent driver.
He's watching TV in the living room.
I need a new cell phone.

AVOID THE *Error*

A complete sentence has a subject and a verb. Ensure each sentence and question has a complete subject and verb.

✘ My two best friends, Bob and Sue, going to the concert with me.

✔ My two best friends, Bob and Sue, **are going** to the concert with me.

- **At the end of an abbreviation**

  I have an appointment with Dr. Sawlani.
  We need 20 lbs. of potatoes.

AVOID THE *Error*

Do not use periods with acronyms. Acronyms are abbreviations formed from the first letters of a name or title. Acronyms are usually pronounced as words.

✗	✓
N.A.S.A. stands for "National Aeronautics and Space Administration."	*NASA* stands for "National Aeronautics and Space Administration." (*NASA* is pronounced "NA-suh.")

Many organizations whose shortened names are not pronounced as words but as individual letters do not use periods after the letters in the shortened names.

✗	✓
A.M.A. stands for "American Medical Association."	*AMA* stands for "American Medical Association." (*AMA* is pronounced A-M-A.)
You need to file your tax return with the **I.R.S.** no later than April 15.	You need to file your tax return with the **IRS** no later than April 15. (*IRS* is pronounced I-R-S.)

If an abbreviation is at the end of a question or exclamation, it's followed by a question mark or exclamation mark.

Did it weigh 20 lbs.?

AVOID THE *Error*

If an abbreviation is at the end of a sentence, you do not need two periods.

✗	✓
He bought apples, oranges, grapes, etc..	He bought apples, oranges, grapes, etc.

The titles *Mr.* and *Mrs.* are abbreviations for full forms that are no longer used. Always use a period after these abbreviations. *Ms.* is not an abbreviation, but it uses a period.

AVOID THE *Error*

With *Miss*, do not use a period.

✗ Miss. Metzger is a teacher in this school.

✔ Miss Metzger is a teacher in this school.

Periods are used in Internet addresses. If an Internet address is at the end of a sentence, use a period at the end. The reader should know not to include that period when using the address online.

My favorite source for news is www.cnn.com.

AVOID THE *Error*

When periods are used in an Internet address (a URL) or an e-mail address, we say *dot*, not *period*.

✗ "w-w-w **period** c-n-n **period** c-o-m"

✔ "w-w-w **dot** c-n-n **dot** c-o-m"

Exclamation Mark

Exclamation marks show emotion and excitement. We often use exclamation marks in imperatives.

Watch out!
I love my new SUV!
Be careful!
I just won $20 million in the lottery!

For more information on imperatives, see page 142.

AVOID THE *Error*

Avoid excessive exclamation marks, especially in more formal kinds of writing, such as business letters. Do not use multiple exclamation marks, except in very informal kinds of writing, such as a letter to a good friend or a message in a greeting card.

✗ Spex Optical is happy to receive your application for employment! You have exactly the qualifications we are looking for! We'd like to set up an interview soon! Please call us right away!

✓ Spex Optical is happy to receive your application for employment. You have exactly the qualifications we are looking for. We'd like to set up an interview soon. Please call us right away.

✗ I really miss you!!! I can't wait for you to get back from your trip!!! See you soon!!!!!

✓ I really miss you. I can't wait for you to get back from your trip. See you soon!

We can use an exclamation point at the end of an imperative or a sentence if it's said with emotion.

You're getting married! Congratulations!

AVOID THE *Error*

An exclamation mark is not required at the end of every imperative. Use an exclamation mark only when the words are said with emotion.

✗ Hand in your test paper when you are finished!

✓ Hand in your test paper when you are finished.

Question Mark

Use a question mark at the end of a direct question.

Who left the door open?
Are you ready to leave yet?

AVOID THE *Error*

Do not use a question mark at the end of an indirect question, which is a question inside of a statement. An indirect question is a part of a statement, so use a period.

✗ I wonder who will win the race?	✓ I wonder who will win the race.
✗ The boss asked who could work late?	✓ The boss asked who could work late.

Comma

We use commas with words, phrases, or clauses that come in a series. Use commas:

- **With three or more items in a series joined by *and* or *or*.** Use a comma when a sentence contains a series of items (nouns, phrases, or clauses) joined by *and*.

He served broccoli, mashed potatoes, **and** carrots with dinner.
They went to the mall, shopped for new clothes, **and** went to the movies.
Alison vacuumed the living room, Tim washed the dishes, Diane cleaned the bathroom, **and** Liz shouted instructions to all of them.

The last comma in the series (before *and*) is optional.

He served broccoli, mashed potatoes and carrots with dinner.

AVOID THE *Error*

Avoid excess commas with items in a series. Do not use a comma:

- With only two items in a series

✗ He applied for the job last week, and has an interview on Monday.	✔ He applied for the job last week and has an interview on Monday.

- Before the first item in a series

✗ You cannot, smoke, chew gum, eat, or drink in the auditorium.	✔ You cannot smoke, chew gum, eat, or drink in the auditorium.

- After the last item in a series

✗ You cannot smoke, chew gum, eat, or drink, in the auditorium.	✔ You cannot smoke, chew gum, eat, or drink in the auditorium.

- After *and* or *or*

✗ They met, dated for two years, got engaged, and, got married two years ago.	✔ They met, dated for two years, got engaged, and got married two years ago.

- **With *such as*.** *Such as* can be used to introduce an example or examples. Use a comma before *such as*.

This summer, I want to learn to cook Italian food**, such as** lasagna, spaghetti, and linguine.

AVOID THE *Error*

Do not use a comma after *such as*.

✗ There are many nice people in my apartment building, such as, Mr. Williams.	✔ There are many nice people in my apartment building, such as Mr. Williams.

- **Between two or more adjectives in a series.** Use a comma between two or more coordinate adjectives in a series. (Coordinate adjectives can have their order changed and can be joined with *and*.)

He bought some ugly red T-shirts. (You cannot say "red ugly T-shirts," so a comma is not needed.)

The intelligent, hardworking students got high grades. (You can say "hardworking, intelligent," so a comma is needed.)

- **Between two independent clauses in a sentence.** Use a comma when two independent clauses are joined into a single sentence with *and, but, or, nor, for, yet,* or *so*. An independent clause has a complete subject and verb and can stand alone as a sentence.

My dog likes to go outside, **and** my cat likes to sleep in front of the fireplace.

He went to the supermarket, **but** he forgot to buy milk.

The mechanic will fix the problem, **or** I will have to buy a new car.

She was locked out of her apartment, **for** she lost her keys on the bus.

He spent the whole day at the water park, **yet** he never got wet.

They didn't check a map before leaving, **so** they got lost almost right away.

AVOID THE *Error*

Do not join two independent clauses with only a comma. This error is often called a "comma splice."

✗ Franklin cut the lawn in the morning, **his** brother cleaned the garage.

Correct a comma splice by joining the clauses with a semicolon or with a comma and *and, but, or, nor, for, yet,* or *so*.

✓ Franklin cut the lawn in the morning, **and** his brother cleaned the garage.

✓ Franklin cut the lawn in the morning; his brother cleaned the garage.

A comma is not needed when the clauses are very short.

She got up and he made breakfast.

AVOID THE *Error*

Do not use a comma to join only two compound elements, such as compound subjects or predicates, or compound objects of prepositions. Compound elements are joined with words such as *and*, *but*, and *or*.

✘ My job involves training salespeople, and observing them in the field.

✔ My job involves training salespeople and observing them in the field.

✘ I am afraid that there is a disagreement between Mary, and Jane.

✔ I am afraid that there is a disagreement between Mary and Jane.

✘ At work today, I mailed some letters, and made some phone calls.

✔ At work today, I mailed some letters and made some phone calls.

- **Between a dependent clause and an independent clause.** Use a comma to join a dependent clause followed by an independent clause. A clause has a complete subject and a complete verb. An independent clause can stand alone. A dependent clause cannot stand alone as a sentence. A subordinating conjunction (such as *when*, *if*, *though*, *while*, etc.) joins the two clauses.

If I win the grand prize in the lottery, I'll buy a new house and a new car.

Though she wasn't hungry, Mavis ate a slice of pizza.

AVOID THE *Error*

Do not use a comma to join an independent clause followed by a dependent clause.

✘ I'll buy a new car and a new house, if I win the lottery.

✔ I'll buy a new car and a new house if I win the lottery.

Other subordinating conjunctions include *so that*, *that*, and *in order that*.

AVOID THE *Error*

Do not confuse *so* with *so that*. *So* introduces an independent clause. A comma is needed before *so*.

✘ He won a million dollars in the lottery **so** he quit his job and moved to Hawaii.	✔ He won a million dollars in the lottery, **so** he quit his job and moved to Hawaii.

So that means "in order that" and introduces a dependent clause. A comma is not needed before *so that*, because a comma is not needed when an independent clause is followed by a dependent clause.

✘ He put his backpack near the front door, **so that** he could find it easily leaving for work.	✔ He put his backpack near the front door **so that** he could find it easily leaving for work.

A comma is needed when the clause with *so that* begins the sentence.

✘ **So that** he wouldn't forget he put his backpack near the front door.	✔ **So that** he wouldn't forget, he put his backpack near the front door.

■ **Before and after an appositive.** An appositive is a noun or noun phrase that uses other words to restate the noun just before it. Commas always come before and after an appositive.

George Washington, **the first president of the United States,** was elected in 1789.

I'd like to introduce my uncle, **Don Mantle**. He owns a used bicycle shop, **Don's Bikes**.

For more information on appositives, see page 56.

■ **After an introductory prepositional phrase.** A prepositional phrase is formed with a preposition and a noun. Prepositional phrases can modify nouns, verbs, or a whole sentence. An introductory prepositional phrase is at the beginning of a sentence and modifies the whole sentence. Use a comma after an introductory prepositional phrase, unless the phrase is very short.

At the beginning of the winter driving season, motorists should check their radiator fluid.

In summer check your coolant. (no comma necessary)

For more information on prepositions and prepositional phrases, see page 238.

- **After an introductory participial phrase.** A present participle is a verb + *-ing*. A past participle is a verb + *-ed*. Participles are used with forms of *be* or *have* to form various tenses. Participles can also be used as modifiers. An introductory participial phrase is formed with a present or past participle and its objects and modifiers. An introductory participial phrase is followed by a comma.

Quickly running downstairs, Dale tripped and fell down.

Bored by the long speeches, Laura and Julie dozed off.

AVOID THE *Error*

A comma is not needed after *but* or *although* when one of these words begins a sentence.

✘ But, he was not able to finish.	✔ But he was not able to finish.
✘ Although, he speaks English exceptionally well, he sometimes misunderstands people.	✔ Although he speaks English exceptionally well, he sometimes misunderstands people.

- **After an introductory adverb.** When an adverb begins a sentence and modifies the whole sentence, it is set off with a comma.

Exceptionally, employees may be granted time off if they make up the time.

AVOID THE *Error*

Do not use a comma after an adverb at the beginning of the sentence if it modifies only one part of the sentence, such as an adjective that follows it.

✘ Exceptionally, delicious Christmas cookies are easy to make.	✔ Exceptionally delicious Christmas cookies are easy to make.

- **Before and after an interrupting phrase.** Use commas before and after a word or phrase that interrupts a sentence.

John wants to go to Florida on vacation. Mary, **however**, wants to go to California.

- **Before and after words in direct address.** Use commas before and after a word that is said in direct address (i.e., said directly to the listener).

Lucy, what did you do to your hair?
I think, **Dale,** that your suggestion is a good one.
Let's go, **everybody!**

- **In dates.** Use a comma between the day and the year in dates.

Today is April 13, 2009.
The United States declared independence from Britain on July 4, 1776.

- **In locations.** Use a comma before and after the state when both city and state appear together.

The Declaration of Independence was signed in Philadelphia, Pennsylvania.
Washington, DC, is the capital of the United States.

AVOID THE Error

Avoid unnecessary commas. Do not use a comma between:

- The subject and the verb

✗ The most careful drivers, always drive defensively. ✓ The most careful drivers always drive defensively.

- A preposition and its object

✗ He tried to fix the drainpipe with, an old pipe wrench. ✓ He tried to fix the drainpipe with an old pipe wrench.

- An adjective and the noun it modifies

✗ We bought some delicious, watermelon for dessert. ✓ We bought some delicious watermelon for dessert.

Colon

Use a colon after an independent clause to introduce a list.

This box contains your new computer equipment: a keyboard, a monitor, a printer, and a mouse.

Trace needs these ingredients to make banana bread: bananas, flour, oil, sugar, salt, and baking powder.

AVOID THE *Error*

Do not use a colon to separate a verb and its objects.

✘ Please buy: apples, oranges, and grapes.

✔ Please buy apples oranges, and grapes.

Use a colon after an independent clause to introduce an idea.

After wandering for hours, they could reach only one conclusion: they were lost.

I have a great suggestion: let's go to the beach on Sunday.

AVOID THE *Error*

Do not use a colon between a preposition and its object or objects.

✘ Tomorrow, I'm going to see a baseball game between: Chicago and St. Louis.

✔ Tomorrow, I'm going to see a baseball game between Chicago and St. Louis.

For more information on prepositions, see page 238.

Semicolon

Use a semicolon to link independent clauses without a coordinating conjunction.

Margo graduated from college; however, she decided to travel for a year before getting a job.

Some people deny that global warming is a problem; most scientists disagree with them.

AVOID THE *Error*

Do not use a semicolon in place of a colon.

✘ Please order these supplies; a box of copier paper, three dozen pens, and ten boxes of paper clips.

✔ Please order these supplies: a box of copier paper, three dozen pens, and ten boxes of paper clips.

Quotation Marks

Use quotation marks for titles of books, movies, stories, TV shows, and so on.

I love watching "Friends."

AVOID THE *Error*

In formal writing, writers use quotation marks for short works (such as stories) and *italics* or <u>underlining</u> for longer works.

✘ The Ransom of Red Chief is a famous story by O. Henry. (a shorter work)

✔ "The Ransom of Red Chief" is a famous story by O. Henry.

✘ <u>**The Ransom of Red Chief**</u> is a famous story by O. Henry.

✘ ***The Ransom of Red Chief*** is a famous story by O. Henry.

✘ Star Wars is my favorite movie. (a longer work)

✔ <u>**Star Wars**</u> is my favorite movie.

✔ ***Star Wars*** is my favorite movie.

In informal writing, quotation marks are acceptable.

✔ "Star Wars" is my favorite movie.

Use quotation marks to show a speaker's exact words.

The bride quietly answered, "I do."
Lincoln's most famous speech begins with the words, "Four score and seven years ago."

AVOID THE *Error*

Always put a period or comma inside the quotation marks.

✗ The groom said, "I do", too. ✓ The groom said, "I do," too.

Place a question mark or exclamation mark inside the quotation marks if it's part of the quotation. If not, place the punctuation mark outside the quotation marks.

✗ "You're late"! she shouted. ✓ "You're late!" she shouted.

✗ Did you watch "The Tonight Show?" ✓ Did you watch "The Tonight Show"?

Use a comma before and after a quotation.

He said, "It's time for lunch."
"Flight 291 for Chicago is ready for passenger boarding," she announced.

Exercises

A *Read each sentence and end each one with a period, question mark, or exclamation mark, as needed.*

1. Can I make an appointment on July 8
2. Watch out for the bee
3. I am going to the library this afternoon
4. Where is the mall
5. I am thinking about selling my car
6. Hurry up or we will be late
7. Would you like to go to a concert next weekend
8. I am so angry I could scream
9. I am cooking spaghetti for dinner tonight
10. I wonder when the movie begins tonight

B *Rewrite the sentences, using correct punctuation.*

1. If I lose my job in a layoff I will go back to school, to become a medical lab technician.

   ____

2. Some cool refreshing ice, cream would taste good right about now, Anne.

   ____

3. Although, the team won the first game of the play-offs they lost the following three games, and were eliminated from the championship.

   ____

4. In winter, you should always wear warm, clothes.

   ____

5. Ali and Fatima have several grown children, they do not have any grandchildren.

   ____

6. I have a suggestion; let's get a new TV for the living room.

   ____

7. John likes to watch movies on TV, his brother likes to rent videos from a store.

   ____

8. Let's sell: brownies, cookies, coffee cake, coffee, and, tea at the bake sale, next weekend.

   ____

9. He got up early exercised, took a shower, and, drove to work, every day last week.

   ____

10. Sonya is very busy these days, she has a full-time job during the week, and a part-time job on Saturdays.

    ____

GRAMMAR

NOUNS

A noun is a word that names a person, place, animal, thing, event, idea, quality, action, or state. Here are examples of each kind of noun:

Person	boy, girl, Bob, Grace, driver
Place	park, Disneyland, supermarket, house, classroom
Animal	dog, cat, robin, elephant, snake
Thing	pencil, computer, bicycle, car, book
Event	World Series, concert, festival
Idea	love, freedom, equality, truth, justice
Quality	excellence, purity, cleanliness
Action	running, eating, working, playing, reading, watching, cooking
State or feeling	happiness, depression, anxiety, boredom, excitement, interest

Singular and Plural

A noun that refers to one thing is singular. A noun that refers to two or more things is plural.

one window	**two** windows
one book	**several** books

Spelling Plural Nouns

To form most plurals, add *-s* or *-es* to the end of the noun.

-S	-ES
pen**s**	bus**es**
car**s**	church**es**
play**s**	countr**ies**
movie**s**	parti**es**

AVOID THE *Error*

Do not use an apostrophe (') when forming a plural noun.

✘ We need some pen's.

✘ We need some pens**'**.

✔ We need some pen**s**.

This table sums up the rules for spelling plural nouns:

FORMING PLURAL NOUNS

SINGULAR	PLURAL
For most nouns, add *-s* to form the plural:	
apple	apple**s**
car	car**s**
dog	dog**s**
cookie	cookie**s**
book	book**s**
For nouns that end in a consonant + *-y*, change the *y* to *i* and add *-es*:	
country	countr**ies**
baby	bab**ies**
party	part**ies**
dictionary	dictionar**ies**
For nouns that end in a vowel + *-y*, add *-s* to the noun:	
guy	guy**s**
boy	boy**s**
key	key**s**
way	way**s**
play	play**s**
Sunday	Sunday**s**
For nouns that end in *-s*, *-ss*, *-x*, *-ch*, and *-sh*, add *-es* to the noun:	
address	address**es**
bus	bus**es**
box	box**es**
fox	fox**es**
church	church**es**
dish	dish**es**
wish	wish**es**

For nouns that end in a consonant + *-o*, add *-es* to the noun:

tomato	tomato**es**
potato	potato**es**

For nouns that end in a vowel + *-o*, add *-s* to the noun:

video	video**s**
kangaroo	kangaroo**s**

For nouns that end in *-fe*, change *f* to *v*, and add *s*:

knife	kni**ves**
life	li**ves**
wife	wi**ves**

For nouns that end in *-f*, change *f* to *v*, and add *-es*:

half	hal**ves**
leaf	lea**ves**
thief	thie**ves**
loaf	loa**ves**

AVOID THE *Error*

There are some exceptions to these rules:

kilo	✘ kilo**es**	✔ kilo**s**
piano	✘ piano**es**	✔ piano**s**
safe	✘ sa**ves**	✔ safe**s** (*safe* is a noun)
roof	✘ roo**ves**	✔ roof**s**
belief	✘ belie**ves**	✔ belief**s**

Only a few nouns end in *-z*, such as *quiz*. Double the final consonant and add *-es*:

quiz**zes**

AVOID THE *Error*

Avoid common spelling errors with regular plurals.

✘ tomatos	✔ tomatoes
✘ potatos	✔ potatoes
✘ babys	✔ babies
✘ knifes	✔ knives

A few nouns only occur in the plural form:

trousers	pants	jeans	(eye)glasses
savings	accommodations	arms (weapons)	stairs

AVOID THE *Error*

Do not use words such as *trousers*, *pants*, *jeans*, and so on in the singular.

✘ He bought a new **jean**. ✔ He bought some new **jeans**.

Some plural nouns are irregular:

man	men
woman	women
child	child**ren**
t**oo**th	t**ee**th
f**oo**t	f**ee**t
m**ouse**	m**ice**

AVOID THE *Error*

Use irregular plurals correctly.

✘ He lost two tooth**s**. ✔ He lost two t**ee**th.

✘ Her foot**s** hurt. ✔ Her f**ee**t hurt.

A few nouns have the same form for the singular and the plural:

fish sheep aircraft

I bought **a new fish** for my fish tank.
I bought **some new fish** for my fish tank.

AVOID THE *Error*

Fish can be made plural only when it refers to many varieties of fishes, especially in science.

✘ Of all the **fish,** the shark is the most feared. ✔ Of all the **fishes,** the shark is the most feared.

Pronouncing Plural Nouns

The plural ending of nouns is pronounced in one of three ways: /əz/, /s/, or /z/. Pronounce the plural ending as:

- /əz/ after /s, z, ʃ, tʃ, ʤ/

  churches judges houses faces quizzes boxes

For information on these phonetic symbols, see pages 3 and 4.

- /s/ after a voiceless consonant such as /f, t, k, p/ (The vocal chords do not vibrate when you say voiceless sounds.)

  bats books chips boats banks stamps

- /z/ after a vowel or a voiced consonant such as /v, d, g, n, m, l/ (The vocal chords vibrate when saying vowels and voiced consonants.)

  parties boys chairs shelves
  cars apples tables tomatoes

For more information on voiced and voiceless sounds, see pages 3 and 4.

Countable and Uncountable Nouns

In English, nouns can be divided into two groups: nouns you can count (countable nouns) and nouns you can't count (uncountable nouns).

Countable Nouns

You can count countable nouns. They have plural forms. You can use the indefinite articles *a* and *some* with countable nouns.

a dog two dogs some dogs
a cat seven cats some cats

Uncountable Nouns

Uncountable nouns include things such as water, meat, cheese, and so on. They are called uncountable because you usually can't count them. You can use the article *the* with uncountable nouns. You can also use the indefinite article *some* with uncountable nouns. But you cannot use the indefinite article *a* with uncountable nouns.

water rice wood information
money cement bread

AVOID THE *Error*

Do not use the indefinite article *a* with uncountable nouns.

✗ Let's buy **a** bread for dinner. ✔ Let's buy **some** bread for dinner.

✗ **A** milk is good to drink. ✔ Milk is good to drink.

Do not use *another*, *every*, *few*, or *many* with uncountable nouns.

✗ **Many** water would be good right now. ✔ **Some** water would be good right now.

✗ I need **another** flour to make the cake. ✔ I need **more** flour to make the cake.

Uncountable nouns do not have plural forms.

AVOID THE *Error*

Do not use plural forms with uncountable nouns.

✗ We bought some bread**s** for dinner. ✔ We bought some bread for dinner.

✗ They washed their hands with soap**s** and water**s**. ✔ They washed their hands with soap and water.

A few words are both countable and uncountable nouns.

I ate some **pizza** for lunch.	I ordered a **pizza** for my family's dinner.
Fried **chicken** is tasty.	Baby **chickens** are called chicks.

AVOID THE *Error*

The words *clothes* and *clothing* have the same meaning, but different usage. *Clothes* is a plural count noun. It does not have a singular form.

✗ I bought **a new clothes** today. My new **clothes looks** great.	✔ I bought **some new clothes** today. My new **clothes look** great.

The related word *cloth* refers to fabric, the material clothing is made from. This word is not the singular form of *clothes*.

✗ I wore my **new cloth** today.	✔ I wore my **new clothes** today.

Cloth is an uncountable noun. Therefore, it doesn't have a plural form.

✗ I bought **some nice cloths** to make new kitchen curtains.	✔ I bought **some nice cloth** to make new kitchen curtains.

Clothing is an uncountable noun.

✗ I am shopping for some **clothings. Clothings are** too expensive.	✔ I am shopping for **some clothing. Clothing is** too expensive.

Using Partitives with Uncountable Nouns

We can use partitive expressions to make uncountable nouns countable. Partitives are words that express containers or units, such as *bottle*, *box*, *loaf*, and so on. Partitives usually are followed by a phrase beginning with *of*, such as "a bottle *of mineral water*." Here are some common partitives:

water	a **bottle** of water	**two bottles** of water
bread	a **loaf** of bread	**some loaves** of bread
candy	a **box** of candy	**several boxes** of candy

Questions with *How Much* and *How Many*

We use *how much* to ask questions about uncountable nouns.

How much flour do you need for that bread recipe?

We use *how many* to ask questions about countable nouns.

How many loaves of bread do you want to make?

Possessive Nouns

A possessive noun shows who or what another noun belongs to.

Megan**'s** book (Megan owns the book.)
the car**'s** door (The door belongs to the car.)

We use an *-s* and an apostrophe (') to form possessive nouns. Follow these rules:

- Add an apostrophe and an *-s* to singular-count nouns.

John**'s** book
the school**'s** new building
the dog**'s** collar

AVOID THE *Error*

To make a singular noun that ends in *-s* or *-es* possessive, do not add only an apostrophe (')—add *'s.*

✘ the bass' voice	✔ the bass's voice

A few words that end in *-s* can add only an apostrophe to form the possessive, such as *Jesus* or a few Greek writers, to avoid an unpleasant repeating of the /s/ sound.

✘ Jesus's teachings	✔ Jesus' teachings
✘ Sophocles's plays	✔ Sophocles' plays

- Add an apostrophe to regular plural count nouns.

the girls' backpacks (two girls have backpacks)
the wheels' new hubcaps

AVOID THE *Error*

Do not add *'s* to regular plural nouns to make them possessive.

✘ the dogs**'s** water bowls	✔ the dog**s'** water bowls
✘ the boys**'s** baseball game	✔ the boys' baseball game

Add *'s* to irregular plurals that do not end in *-s*.

the women**'s** room　　　the men**'s** room

AVOID THE *Error*

Do not add *the* before a possessive proper noun.

✗ I want to see **the** Mary's new car.

✓ I want to see Mary's new car.

✗ **The** Thrifty Bank's new drive-through window is open seven days a week.

✓ Thrifty Bank's new drive-through window is open seven days a week.

You can use *the* with a possessive proper noun when *the* is part of the noun.

✓ This year, **the** Boy Scouts' annual holiday wreath sale will be December 10–23.

We can also form possessives with an *of* phrase and a possessive noun.

Raymond is a neighbor **of Tim's**.

AVOID THE *Error*

When we use possessives with a phrase with *of*, use a possessive noun.

✗ A book **of Allen** is lost.

✓ A book **of Allen's** is lost.

However, when we use an *of* phrase following a person, the object of *of* can be a noun or a possessive.

✓ A friend **of John** is coming to the party.
✓ A friend **of John's** is coming to the party.

Use *whose* to ask questions about possessive nouns.

Whose car is parked in front of the house?
Whose phone rang in the middle of the wedding?
Whose keys are these?

AVOID THE *Error*

Do not confuse *whose* (question word) with *who's* (abbreviation of question word *who* + *is*).

✘ **Who's** book is this? ✔ **Whose** book is this?

✘ **Whose** your favorite singer? ✔ **Who's** your favorite singer?

Comparing Nouns

We use *fewer . . . than*, *the fewest*, *less . . . than*, and *the least* to compare quantities of nouns. Use *fewer . . . than* and *the fewest* with countable nouns.

We have **fewer** apples **than** oranges.
We have **the fewest** grapefruit.

Use *less . . . than* and *the least* with uncountable nouns.

We have **less** salt **than** sugar.
We have **the least** pepper.

Appositives

An appositive is a noun that restates another noun in new or different words.

Abraham Lincoln, **the sixteenth president**, ended the Civil War.
My best friend, **Ray**, works downtown.

AVOID THE *Error*

An appositive must refer to the noun it precedes or follows.

✘ A talented singer, they hired Susan Alexander to perform in the opera.

To correct a misplaced appositive, move it nearer to the noun or rewrite the sentence.

✔ They hired Susan Alexander, **a talented singer**, to perform in the opera.

✔ A talented singer, **Susan Alexander**, was hired to perform in the opera.

Exercises

A *Write the plural form of each word.*

1. cheeseburger ____________________
2. sandwich ____________________
3. party ____________________
4. cowboy ____________________
5. wife ____________________
6. room ____________________
7. tomato ____________________
8. match ____________________
9. orange ____________________
10. foot ____________________
11. mouse ____________________
12. box ____________________
13. glass ____________________
14. zoo ____________________
15. apple ____________________
16. man ____________________
17. roof ____________________
18. tooth ____________________
19. video ____________________
20. life ____________________

B *Complete the sentences by using* some *and the noun in parentheses. Make the countable nouns plural.*

1. ____________________ (**child**) are playing baseball in the park.
2. Do you want ____________________ (**milk**) with your sandwich?
3. I bought ____________________ (**orange**) at the fruit market this morning.
4. There are ____________________ (**towel**) in the closet.
5. Let's serve ____________________ (**cheese**) at the party.
6. I think that the post office just delivered ____________________ (**box**) for you.

7. Next summer, I want to plant __________________ (**flower**) in front of the house.
8. Every day, I get __________________ (**bill**) in the mail.
9. The doctor said that Tracy needs to get __________________ (**exercise**) every day.
10. The teacher gave the class __________________ (**homework**) last night.

C *Complete the shopping list. Choose an appropriate word to complete the sentence, making the word plural if necessary. If the noun in the shopping list is a countable noun, make it plural.*

bag bag bottle box box loaf

1. One ____________ of cornflake _______
2. Three ____________ of water _______
3. One ____________ of candy _______
4. One ____________ of barbecue potato chip _______
5. Three ____________ of bread _______
6. One ____________ of cookie _______

D *Write the possessive form of the word in parentheses.*

1. I believe that this is ____________(**Anne**) book.
2. Where is the ____________ (**women**) restroom?
3. Let's paint the ____________ (**boys**) bedroom this weekend.
4. Please meet me in the ____________ (**teachers**) lounge at 11:00.
5. We are invited to ____________ (**Tony**) house for a picnic.

E *How do you pronounce the plural ending? Write /s/, /z/, or /əz/ on the line.*

1. girls _______
2. cats _______
3. pencils _______
4. potatoes _______
5. bottles _______
6. quizzes _______

7. cups ________
8. books ________
9. glasses ________
10. shelves ________

F *Complete the questions by writing* How much, How many, *or* Whose *on the line.*

1. ____________________ people work in your office?
2. ____________________ apples do you want?
3. ____________________ fried chicken should we order?
4. ____________________ cars were in the accident?
5. ____________________ money does it cost?
6. ____________________ books are on the kitchen table, John's or Laura's?
7. ____________________ water should we buy?
8. ____________________ chair is this?

NUMBERS

Cardinal Numbers

1	one
2	two
3	three
4	four
5	five
6	six
7	seven
8	eight
9	nine
10	ten
11	eleven
12	twelve
13	thirteen
14	fourteen
15	fifteen
16	sixteen
17	seventeen
18	eighteen
19	nineteen
20	twenty
30	thirty
40	forty
50	fifty
60	sixty
70	seventy
80	eighty
90	ninety
100	one hundred
1,000	one thousand

10,000	ten thousand
100,000	one hundred thousand
1,000,000	one million
1,000,000,000	one billion

Decimals and Fractions

$\frac{1}{2}$	one-half
$\frac{1}{3}$	one-third
$\frac{2}{3}$	two-thirds
$\frac{3}{4}$	three-fourths, or three-quarters
$\frac{1}{6}$	one-sixth
0.1	one-tenth
0.2	two-tenths
0.01	one-hundredth
0.21	twenty-one hundredths

Ordinal Numbers

1st	first
2nd	second
3rd	third
4th	fourth
5th	fifth
6th	sixth
7th	seventh
8th	eighth
9th	ninth
10th	tenth

Writing and Saying Cardinal Numbers

We use cardinal numbers to count. Most numbers are written in the same way around the world.

AVOID THE Error

There are two differences in how North Americans and Europeans write numbers:

- North Americans write **1** with a single stroke. In Europe and many other places, this number has an additional stroke.
- In Europe and other places, people write the number **7** with an additional stroke. North Americans do not use this additional stroke.
- Do not use extra strokes with the numbers **1** and **7** in North America.

✔ North America: I 7

✔ Europe and other parts of the world: 1 7

Zero

For the number *zero*, people say "zero" or "oh." In ordinary speech, people usually say "oh" for zero.

Odd and Even Numbers

Odd numbers are numbers that cannot be divided evenly by two. Even numbers can be divided evenly by two.

Even: 0, 2, 4, 6, 8
Odd: 1, 3, 5, 7

So when an English speaker mentions an odd number, he or she doesn't mean the number is strange or unusual. The person means that the number can't be divided evenly by two.

Dozen

Dozen means "twelve." *Baker's dozen* means "thirteen." This comes from a common practice of bakers giving a free item when the customer buys twelve. English speakers often use *dozen* to describe an approximate number.

Dozens of people were inconvenienced when the bus broke down.

Tens and Teens

To clearly say numbers such as *thirteen* and *thirty*, stress the last syllable of numbers ending in *-teen* (such as ***thirteen***), but stress the first syllable of numbers ending in *-ty* (such as ***thirty***).

thir**teen**	**thir**ty
four**teen**	**for**ty
fif**teen**	**fif**ty

In general, we say numbers in groups of hundreds, tens, and ones.

145	one hundred forty-five
76	seventy-six

We can shorten numbers from 101–999 by leaving off the word *hundred*.

101	one-oh-one
145	one forty-five
913	nine thirteen

AVOID THE *Error*

Do not use *and* before the last word of a number.

✘ two hundred twenty **and** nine	✔ two hundred twenty-nine
✘ two hundred **and** twenty-nine	✔ two twenty-nine

Using Numbers and Number Words

In informal writing, such as notes and e-mails, use numbers for all numbers. In formal writing, such as reports for school or business letters, use number words for numbers you can write in one or two words. Use numbers for larger or more complicated numbers.

This table shows when to use numbers or number words in more formal kinds of writing:

USE NUMBER WORDS	USE NUMBERS
twenty books	151 books
forty-five boxes	314 boxes
thirty pounds	35.2 pounds
one-half	$1\frac{1}{5}$
six percent	6.25%

AVOID THE *Error*

In formal writing, always use number words when a number is first in a sentence. If the number is very long, rewrite the sentence so the number is not at the beginning of the sentence.

✘ 23% of this ice cream is fat.

✔ Twenty-three percent of this ice cream is fat.

✔ This ice cream is 23% fat.

Writing and Saying Larger Numbers

Say longer numbers in groups of ten thousands, thousands, hundreds, and so on. When you write longer numbers, use commas to separate groups of three numbers.

WRITE	SAY
19,245	nineteen thousand two hundred forty-five

AVOID THE *Error*

Do not use a period to separate groups of numbers in a larger number—use a comma.

✘ 1.204.196

✔ 1,204,196

The largest numbers frequently used in everyday speech are *million* (1,000,000) and *billion* (1,000,000,000). A *millionaire* is a person who has at least a million dollars. A *billionaire* has at least a billion dollars. Larger numbers, such as *trillion* (1,000,000,000,000), are rarely used.

AVOID THE *Error*

You may hear English speakers use words such as *zillion* or *gazillion* to refer to very large numbers or amounts. These words express a large quantity or number, but they are *not* actual numbers. Do not use these numbers in formal speech or writing.

✘ The federal budget deficit is more than a zillion dollars.

✔ The federal budget deficit is in the billions of dollars.

Write and say very large approximate numbers this way:

WRITE	SAY
20 million	twenty million
110 billion	one hundred ten billion

AVOID THE *Error*

Do not make the words *million* and *billion* plural when they are accompanied by a number.

✗ 20 millions people ✓ 20 million people

You can use *millions* and *billions* when they are not accompanied by a specific number:

✓ Each year, millions of people visit Disney World.

✓ McDonald's has served billions of hamburgers worldwide over the years.

Decimals and Fractions

We use decimals and fractions for numbers smaller than one and greater than zero.

$\frac{1}{2}$ $\frac{2}{3}$ 0.5

Follow these rules for writing and saying decimals and fractions:

- When saying numbers with a fraction, we say *and* before the fraction.

  You see: $2\frac{3}{4}$
  You say: two **and** three-fourths

- When a number includes the fraction $\frac{1}{2}$, we say *a* or *one.*

  You see: $5\frac{1}{2}$
  You say: five and **a** half *or* five **and** one-half

- For decimals (except money), we can use *and* or the word *point.*

  You see: 2.2
  You say: two **and** two-tenths *or* two **point** two

- For numbers less than one, we can say *point* or omit it. We can also say *oh* (for zero) or omit it.

  You see: 0.3
  You say: oh **point** three, **point** three, *or* three-tenths

AVOID THE *Error*

When writing decimal fractions, use a decimal point (.), not a comma.

✗ 98,6 ✓ 98.6

Amounts of Money

In general, people say amounts of money in groups indicating dollars and cents. Join the dollars and cents groups with **and**.

WRITE	SAY
$525	five hundred twenty-five dollars
$719.95	seven hundred nineteen dollars **and** ninety-five cents

However, people sometimes leave off the words *dollars* and *cents* and some of the number words, especially when it's clear they are talking about money.

$19.95	nineteen ninety-five
$27.13	twenty-seven thirteen

When the amount of cents is less than ten, we can say the number of cents in two ways:

Twenty-nine dollars and three cents
Twenty-nine oh three

The value of U.S. coins in numbers does not appear on all coins. U.S. coins have special names, but they appear only on some coins. The size of a coin does not indicate relative value, either. Nickels are bigger than dimes, but they are worth less. Dimes are slightly smaller than pennies, but they are worth more. The following table gives the value of each coin:

COIN NAME	VALUE
penny	one cent
nickel	five cents
dime	ten cents
quarter	twenty-five cents

In everyday speech, a popular slang expression for *dollar* is *buck*. People use this word in friendly, casual conversation.

Hey, you owe me five **bucks** for lunch!
I just won fifty **bucks** in the lottery! Let's go out for pizza!

Telephone Numbers

In general, people say telephone numbers as single numbers, with a very short pause after each group of numbers,

(773) 555-4175	seven-seven-three (pause) five-five-five (pause) four-one-seven-five

Phone numbers with many zeros may be pronounced differently, especially if the number is for a large company.

555-2300	five-five-five (pause) two three hundred
555-8000	five-five-five (pause) eight thousand

Addresses

In general, people say addresses as follows:

NUMBERS	WRITE	SAY
1–99	12 State Street	Twelve State Street
100	100 North Avenue	One hundred North Avenue
101–999	113 Hill Street	One one three Hill Street One thirteen Hill Street
hundreds	900 Michigan Avenue	Nine hundred Michigan Avenue
thousands	1000 Broadway	One thousand Broadway
over 1000	4250 Ocean Boulevard	Forty-two fifty Ocean Boulevard

AVOID THE *Error*

In street addresses, write the building number before the street name, not after it. Do not use a comma between the building number and street name.

✗ 26, Fifth Avenue ✓ 26 Fifth Avenue

✗ Fifth Avenue, 26

Time

In general, you can spell out the time in whole hours (e.g., *five o'clock*) or use numbers (5:00) when you are writing sentences. Write the time in numbers when you want to emphasize a specific time.

I always get up at **5 o'clock** in the morning.
I always get up at **five o'clock** in the morning.
The first bus leaves at **5:41** in the morning.

AVOID THE *Error*

When we state in a sentence the time of an appointment or a departure, we use *at*, not *to*.

✗ The train leaves **to** 12:20. ✓ The train leaves **at** 12:20.

In date books and schedules, always write the time in numbers.

SCHEDULE FOR SATURDAY

9:30 Dentist
10:30 Go to bank, post office, and supermarket
12:00 Meet David for lunch

In informal writing, you can express time in whole hours with or without ":00". If the meaning is clear, you can also omit *o'clock*.

Let's leave at **9**. Let's leave at **9:00**. Let's leave at **9 o'clock**.

AVOID THE *Error*

When saying the time written with ":00", you do not need to say anything for ":00". Just state the hour and *o'clock* if it's needed for clarity.

You see: 9:00

You say:

✗ nine zero-zero o'clock ✓ nine o'clock

✓ nine

Here are some common ways of saying the time:

TIME	WE SAY
10:00	ten o'clock
10:10	ten ten, ten after ten
10:15	(a) quarter past ten, (a) quarter after ten; ten fifteen
10:30	ten thirty, half past ten
10:45	(a) quarter to eleven, (a) quarter 'til eleven, ten forty-five
12:00 (P.M.)	noon, twelve noon, 12 o'clock
12:00 (A.M.)	midnight, twelve midnight, 12 o'clock midnight

AVOID THE *Error*

O'clock is always written with an apostrophe. It's a contraction of *of the clock*, but no one says the full form.

✗ It's 10 **oclock**. ✓ It's ten **o'clock**.

Use *o'clock* with the time only when the time is a full hour.

✗ It's 3:30 o'clock. ✓ It's 3:30.

✓ It's three o'clock.

Use *A.M.* for times from 12:00 midnight to 11:59 in the morning. Use *P.M.* for times from 12:00 noon to 11:59 at night.

Please be at work at 9:30 **A.M.** sharp!
The restaurant opens at 11 **A.M.** and closes at 11 **P.M.**

AVOID THE *Error*

Unlike many countries, the United States does not use a twenty-four-hour system to write the time. For example, in many parts of the world "4 P.M." is written "16:00". Always write the hours in numbers from 1 to 12, and use *A.M.* and *P.M.* to clarify whether the time is before or after noon.

✘ Please be here at 21:00.

✔ Please be here at **9:00 P.M.**

You will see the *A.M.* written with and without periods. Both styles are correct.

Your appointment is at 9:00 **AM** tomorrow.

Your appointment is at 9:00 **A.M.** tomorrow.

AVOID THE *Error*

Many English speakers confuse 12:00 A.M. (midnight) and 12:00 P.M. (noon).

✘ He ate lunch at 12:00 **A.M.**

✔ He ate lunch at 12:00 **P.M.**

✘ Cinderella stayed out dancing until 12:00 **P.M.**

✔ Cinderella stayed out dancing until 12:00 **A.M.**

To tell the difference, remember that we eat lunch in the afternoon (P.M.).

To say approximate times, use *about*, *almost*, *around*, or *nearly*.

It's **nearly** 8 o'clock.
Let's eat dinner at **about** 6:00.

AVOID THE *Error*

Almost and *nearly* can be used only after the verb *be* or the preposition *until.*

✘ We left at **almost** 8:00.

✔ We left at **about** 8:00.

✔ We didn't leave **until almost** 8:00.

✘ He came home at **nearly** midnight.

✔ It was **nearly** midnight when he came home.

✔ He didn't come home **until nearly** midnight.

Using Ordinal Numbers

We use ordinal numbers to show order. We usually write ordinal numbers in number words when we talk about the order of events.

Megan finished **first** in the marathon.

In casual writing, we can use numbers.

She won **2nd** place in the contest!

Dates

We use a mixture of ordinal and cardinal numbers to write and say dates. Use cardinal numbers to write the day. Use ordinal numbers to say the day. This table shows how to write and say dates:

WRITE	SAY
February 19	February nineteenth
July 15	July fifteenth
December 25	December twenty-fifth

AVOID THE *Error*

Do not use ordinal numbers to write the date.

✘ I arrived in the United States on May 20**th**, 2008.

✔ I arrived in the United States on May 20, 2008.

When writing the complete date, write:

- The month
- The day in cardinal numbers
- A comma
- The year in cardinal numbers

July 15, 2008 February 19, 2010

Say years in two groups of numbers.

1958	nineteen fifty-eight
1999	nineteen ninety-nine
1776	seventeen seventy-six

People say years in the twenty-first century in two ways:

2001	two thousand one *or* twenty oh-one

This table shows how to write and say dates:

WRITE	SAY
July 4, 1776	July fourth, seventeen seventy-six
July 8, 2009	July eighth, two thousand nine
July 15, 1958	July fifteenth, nineteen fifty-eight

AVOID THE *Error*

In the United States, people do not write the day before the month when writing dates. Take care to write dates in this order: the month, the day, a comma, and the year.

✗ 20 July 2009 ✓ July 20, 2009

You can also write the date with slashes and numbers: 7/20/2009. You can leave off the first two digits of the year, as long as the meaning is clear: 7/20/09.

In the United States, Independence Day is written in words or number words when it refers to the holiday. To save space, often the ordinal number is used in posters and announcements of holiday events.

People love to watch fireworks on the **Fourth** of July.
People love to watch fireworks on the **4th** of July.

Centuries

Use ordinal numbers to say centuries.

We live in the **twenty-first** century.
George W. Bush was elected president at the end of the **twentieth** century.

Exercises

A *How do you say the numbers? Write each number in words.*

1. 16 children ____________________
2. 235 Redfield Court ____________________
3. January 15, 2010 ____________________
4. (212) 555-1212 ____________________
5. $29.95 ____________________
6. 14% ____________________
7. 101.2 ____________________
8. $17\frac{3}{4}$ ____________________
9. 12:04 A.M. ____________________
10. 6:00 A.M. ____________________

B *Write the sentences correctly.*

1. 10% of the workers were absent yesterday.

____

2. Income tax is due on fifteenth April of each year.

____

3. My address is 336, Rose Avenue.

____

4. The total cost for your new car is $26.419,45.

____

5. Please be at the train station at exactly six-sixteen o'clock in the morning.

____

6. You need six and three-quarter cups of flour for this bread recipe.

____

7. Please remember to buy one hundred forty-six new books to use as graduation presents.

____

8. 5:30 is very early to get up every day.

____

9. She won 1 prize in the cooking contest.

____

10. 31 October is the date of Halloween.

____

DETERMINERS

Determiners are words that come before adjectives and nouns. They include *a/an*, *some*, *the*, *this*, *that*, *these*, and *those*. Determiners tell whether we are talking about a specific noun or a kind of noun in general.

He wiped **the** badly cracked windshield with **a** grimy, old rag.
We cooked **some** delicious vegetarian fried rice **this** morning.
That handsome young gentleman is my nephew.
Please put **these** new wooden chairs with **those** old reading tables at **the** other end of **the** room.

For more information on the order of words before a noun, see page 103.

A/An

A/An means "one thing or person." You can use *a* or *an* before a singular countable noun.

I just bought **a** new car.
Mrs. Wallace is **a** very nice neighbor.
I received **a** nice birthday present from my sister.
I'd like **a** double cheeseburger, please.
Look! **An** elephant!

For more information on countable and uncountable nouns, see page 51.

AVOID THE *Error*

Use *the* after a second reference to the same noun. Do not repeat *a*.

✘ I saw a car drive down the street. **A** car was driving very quickly.

✔ I saw a car drive down the street. **The** car was driving very quickly.

Use *a/an* to say what something or someone is.

A Porsche is **an** expensive car.
A Lhasa Apso is **a** kind of dog from Tibet.
Morocco is **a** country in Africa.
Sue is **a** professor.

AVOID THE *Error*

Do not omit *a* or *an* when stating someone's profession.

✘ He's cab driver. ✔ He's **a** cab driver.

Use *a* or *one* interchangeably before the numbers *hundred*, *thousand*, *hundred thousand*, *million*, and *billion* when referring to either those exact amounts or a number that is near (approximately) one of these numbers.

That company lost more than **a/one** hundred thousand dollars in the stock market yesterday.
That watch costs over **a/one** thousand dollars.
We need **a/one** hundred more boxes of cookies for the cookie sale.

AVOID THE *Error*

In situations other than numbers such as *hundred* and so on, do not substitute *one* for *a*.

✘ He is **one** teacher. ✔ He is **a** teacher.

✘ Please bring me **one** doughnut. ✔ Please bring me **a** doughnut.

Use *one* only to give emphasis to the number.

✔ Please bring me **one** doughnut, not two.

If you give special stress (loudness) to the word *one*, you can say:

✔ Please bring me **one** doughnut.

Use *a* + *day* to talk about the day.

Today is **a** beautiful late September **day**.

AVOID THE *Error*

Use *one day* to talk about an indeterminate day in the past.

✘ **A day** last September, it rained for ten hours without stopping.

✔ **One day** last September, it rained for ten hours without stopping.

Use *a* to talk about prices by weight, such as per-pound prices.

Cheddar cheese is on sale for $2 **a** pound.
Bananas are only 33 cents **per** pound this week.

AVOID THE *Error*

Do not use *the* to talk about prices per pound, ounce, and so on. Use *a*.

✘ Peas are 69 cents **the** pound.

✔ Peas are 69 cents **a** pound.

Choosing Between *A* and *An*

Follow these rules for choosing between *a* and *an*.

- In general, use *a* before a consonant and *an* before a vowel.

I'd like **a** salad and **a** large orange juice, please.
Please give me **an** apple and **an** orange.

- Use *an* before a silent initial *h*. Words with silent *h* include *hour*, *honor*, *herb*, and *honest*.

Please be ready to leave in **an** hour.
It's **an** honor to meet you.

- Use *a* before certain vowels that sound like the consonant sound /y/.

He graduated from **a** university in California.
She is from **a** European country.

AVOID THE *Error*

Another is one word, not two. It means "a different."

✗ This CD-ROM won't work. Please give me **an other** CD-ROM.	✓ This CD-ROM won't work. Please give me **another** CD-ROM.

Some

Some means "an amount of something." Use *some* with uncountable nouns and plural countable nouns.

I'd like **some** orange juice.
John sent his wife **some** flowers on Valentine's Day.

AVOID THE *Error*

Never use *a* or *an* with uncountable nouns. Use *some.*

✗ I bought a flour.	✓ I bought **some** flour.

We can use *some* to mean "a few" or "not all."

I like **some** cats. (I don't like all cats.)

AVOID THE *Error*

The following nouns are uncountable in English but not in many other languages: *bread*, *news*, *information*, *furniture*, *work*, *research*, and *spaghetti*. Do not use *a* with these nouns. Use *some*, and do not make these nouns plural.

✘ Please buy **a** bread when you are at the supermarket.

✔ Please buy **some** bread when you are at the supermarket.

✘ Please buy **some** bread**s** when you are at the supermarket.

Do not confuse *job* and *work*. *Job* is a countable noun that means "an employment" or "a task." *Work* is an uncountable noun. When we use *work* with an article such as *some* or *this*, this word refers to tasks we have to do. We can use *work* without an article to mean "a job."

✘ I need to find **a** work.

✔ I need to find work.

✔ I need to find a job.

✘ We need to get **a** work done before lunch.

✔ We need to get **this** work done before lunch.

✔ My boss just gave me **some** more work to do.

To ask questions about a word preceded by *some,* use *any* in place of *some.*

Do you have **any** pens?
Do we need **any** apples?

In informal English, we can use *some* in these questions, usually with the idea that the answer is affirmative.

Do we have **some** apples?

The

We use *the* to refer to one unique person, place, or thing.

I need to go to **the** bank, **the** post office, and **the** library.
The cashier gave me too much change.

AVOID THE *Error*

Do not use *the* with names of people.

✘ **The** Mr. Smith is my boss. ✔ Mr. Smith is my boss.

✘ **The** Evelyn is a very hard worker. ✔ Evelyn is a very hard worker.

Use *the* with *doctor* and *dentist* when referring to a certain doctor or dentist but not using his or her name.

The doctor will see you now.
The doctor says I should get more rest.

AVOID THE *Error*

Do not use *the* with *Dr.* + name.

✘ I have an appointment with **the** Dr. Alford tomorrow. ✔ I have an appointment with Dr. Alford tomorrow.

Use *the* with kinds of entertainment.

Tim loves to go to **the** opera and **the** movies.

AVOID THE *Error*

Do not use *the* with *TV* when *TV* refers to entertainment or to TV programs. Use *the* only when referring to the electrical appliance.

✘ I'm tired of watching **the** TV. Please turn off TV. ✔ I'm tired of watching TV. Please turn off **the** TV.

Use *the* with organizations.

Tom went camping with **the** Boy Scouts this weekend.
She joined **the** army when she graduated from high school.

AVOID THE *Error*

Do not use *the* when referring to organizations' acronyms. An acronym is an abbreviation that is said as a word.

✘ He works for **the** UNESCO. ✔ He works for UNESCO.

Use *the* with rivers, seas, and oceans.

The Mississippi is the longest river in the United States.
I've never seen **the** Pacific Ocean.

AVOID THE *Error*

Do not use *the* with lakes.

✘ **The** Lake Michigan is in North America. ✔ Lake Michigan is in North America.

Do not use *the* for most countries.

He lives in **England**.
Vietnam is in Southeast Asia.

AVOID THE *Error*

Use *the* with countries that have words such as *kingdom*, *republic*, or *states* in them.

✘ I am from United States. ✔ I am from **the** United States.

✘ "People's Republic of China" is the official name of China. ✔ "**The** People's Republic of China" is the official name of China.

Use *the* with plural countries.

He lives in **the** Bahamas.
I am from **the** Netherlands.

The is part of the name of a few countries. In these cases, *the* is capitalized.

He is from **The Gambia.**

AVOID THE *Error*

Barbados ends with an *-s*, but does not use *the*.

✘ She is from **the** Barbados. ✔ She is from Barbados.

Use *the* when talking about mountain ranges.

The highest peaks in **the** Rocky Mountains are often covered in snow, even in summer.

AVOID THE *Error*

Do not use *the* to talk about individual mountains.

✘ Her dream is to climb **the** Mt. Everest. ✔ Her dream is to climb Mt. Everest.

Use *the* to talk about something that is one of a kind in our solar system.

The sun is behind a cloud right now.
The moon will rise at 8:51 tonight.

AVOID THE *Error*

Do not use *the* for planets. Use *the* for galaxies.

✘ Earth is in Milky Way. ✔ Earth is in **the** Milky Way.

✘ **The** Uranus is the eighth planet. ✔ Uranus is the eighth planet.

Some English speakers use *the* with *Earth*.

✔ Earth is the third planet from the sun.

✔ **The** Earth is the third planet from the sun.

Use *the* with superlatives.

This is **the** most expensive perfume in the world.

For more information on superlatives, see page 105.

AVOID THE *Error*

Use *the* with the word *same* when two things are similar or identical.

✗ I can't tell the difference between regular and extra spicy fried chicken. They taste same to me.

✔ I can't tell the difference between regular and extra spicy fried chicken. They taste **the** same to me.

Use *the* to make a general statement about a singular countable noun.

The rose is a beautiful flower.

AVOID THE *Error*

When *country* means "rural area," we use *the*, not *a*.

✗ I spent the holidays in a country.

✔ I spent the holidays in **the** country.

Use *the* with specific foods and drinks.

The tea smells delicious.

AVOID THE *Error*

Do not use *the* with meals.

✗ **The** breakfast was delicious.

✔ Breakfast was delicious.

Use *the* with nationalities.

The British settled North America.
The French are famous for excellent cooking.
The ancient Greeks invented democratic government.

AVOID THE *Error*

Do not use *the* with languages.

✗ **The** Spanish is an easy language to learn.

✓ Spanish is an easy language to learn.

Zero Article

A noun with a zero article has no article.

He ordered ham and eggs.
I smell roses.
Do you want coffee or tea?
He has lots of luggage.

Use the zero article with an uncountable noun or a plural countable noun when the noun has a general meaning.

Fresh bread smells delicious.
Flowers grow in spring.
Let's make **cookies** tomorrow.

Use the zero article with meals, sports and games, cities, countries, and towns.

What do you want for **breakfast**?
I like to watch **baseball** and **play basketball**.
He lives in **Paris, France**.
Let's play **cards** tonight.

The is used with a few countries. For information, see page 82.

Use the zero article with languages.

He speaks **Spanish**.
Joe knows **Chinese**.

Use the zero article with prepositions and places such as *church*, *school*, *bed*, *prison*, and *home* when the meaning of the sentence implies the person is there to pray, study, sleep, and so on.

He is at **school** all day.	They are playing basketball at **the school.**
He is in **bed** asleep.	Don't put your dirty shoes on **the bed**.
He is at **home** watching TV.	He sold **the home** for $100,000.

Use the zero article with days, months, or expressions such as *last week*.

Next week we will have a test.
Your appointment is on **Monday**.

AVOID THE *Error*

Articles with the names of sicknesses are complicated.

- Use *a/an* with *cold*, *headache*, and *fever*.

✗ I have fever.	✓ I have **a** fever.

- Use *the* with *flu*.

✗ He's sick in bed with flu.	✓ He's sick in bed with **the** flu.

- Use the zero article with *diabetes*, *high blood pressure*, and *hepatitis*.

✗ **The** high blood pressure can be a life-threatening condition.	✓ High blood pressure can be a life-threatening condition.

This, *That*, *These*, and *Those*

Use *this*, *that*, *these*, and *those* + noun to talk about specific objects or people that are near or far. *This* and *that* are singular; *these* and *those* are plural. Use *this* and *these* for nearby objects or people; use *that* and *those* for distant people or objects. This table summarizes the meaning of *this*, *that*, *these*, and *those*:

	NEAR	FAR
Singular	this	that
Plural	these	those

AVOID THE *Error*

You may hear some people use the improper form *them* in place of *these* and *those*. The correct forms are *these* and *those*.

✗ Please put **them** boxes over here.
✓ Please put **those** boxes over here.

✗ **Them** green beans are delicious.
✓ **These** green beans are delicious.

Here are some examples of *this*, *that*, *these*, and *those*.

Would you like **this** baked potato?
These French fries are too salty.
I never want to visit **that** town again!
Please take **those** shirts to the laundromat.

AVOID THE *Error*

This, *that*, *these*, and *those* should agree in number with the nouns they go with. If the noun is singular or uncountable, use *this* or *that*. If the noun is plural, use *these* or *those*. Be careful to use the correct form when modifiers come between the demonstrative adjective and the noun.

✗ Please give me some of **that** barbecue potato chips.
✓ Please give me some of **those** barbecue potato chips.

This, *that*, *these*, and *those* are also used as pronouns. See page 97 for more information.

Exercises

A *Write* a *or* an *on the line.*

1. I would bring ______________ extra pen to the test.
2. I bought ______________ large bottle of water to take on the trip.
3. The movie begins in half ______________ hour.
4. He studied at ______________ European university.
5. Right now he is reading ______________ history of the Civil War.

B *Write* a/an *or* some *on the line.*

1. We need ______________ flour, oil, and salt to fry the fish.
2. Let's send her ______________ big bunch of flowers for her birthday.
3. Scientists in California have discovered ______________ new kind of orchid.
4. Please buy ______________ pens and pencils at the store.
5. The artist painted ______________ beautiful picture of the sunset.
6. I met ______________ friendly college students at the swimming pool.
7. I need to complain to the phone company. My bill has ______________ calls that I didn't make.
8. This weekend there is ______________ free concert in the park.
9. Let's buy ______________ coffee to drink in the car.
10. Picasso was ______________ artist.

C *Write* the *or* zero *on the line.*

1. I asked a man for directions. ______________ man told me to walk north three blocks and turn right.
2. On the sixtieth wedding anniversary it's traditional to give ______________ diamonds as a present.
3. Doctors say that ______________ gum is terrible for your teeth.
4. My uncle says that he wants to retire in ______________ Bahamas.
5. Let's play ______________ baseball after work.
6. He has a bad case of ______________ flu and won't be at work for several days.
7. Rhode Island is ______________ smallest state in the United States.
8. I have to be at work early on ______________ Thursday.
9. Could you open ______________ window, please? It's hot in here.
10. I have to cut ______________ lawn this weekend.

D *Complete the sentence by circling the correct word.*

1. (**This/Those**) apples are delicious.
2. Let's move (**this/that**) couch to the basement. (far)
3. (**These/That**) concert was great.
4. Please put your coat in (**this/that**) closet. (near)
5. (**This/Those**) computer is not working.

PRONOUNS

Pronouns take the place of nouns. Pronouns include *I*, *you*, *he*, *she*, *it*, *we*, *they*, *me*, *him*, *her*, *us*, and *them*. We use pronouns such as *he*, *she*, *it*, and *them* to avoid repeating nouns. We use the pronouns *I*, *you*, *we*, *me*, and *us* to refer directly to people who are present in a place or situation. A pronoun has the same meaning as the noun it replaces or refers to.

I think that **we** are ready to begin. Are **you** ready, too? (*I*, *we*, and *you* refer to people who are present while the speaker is talking.)
Chuck is a good friend of mine. **He** lives in Chicago.
Tom visited **Barcelona**. **It's** a beautiful city.
Mary Jane likes these **shoes**. **She** wants to buy **them**.
Mark only has a little cut. Mark didn't hurt **himself** badly.

These are the subject, object, and reflexive pronouns in English:

SUBJECT	OBJECT	REFLEXIVE
I	me	myself
you	you	yourself, yourselves
he	him	himself
she	her	herself
it	it	itself
we	us	ourselves
they	them	themselves

One is an indefinite subject pronoun. *Oneself* is an indefinite reflexive pronoun. They are used for making general statements that are used in more formal contexts.

One needs to be careful going out late at night.
It's easy to hurt **oneself** on a large waterslide.

In most settings, especially informal ones, English speakers use *you* to make general statements. In these statements, *you* refers to people in general, not to the listener.

You need to be careful going out late at night.
It's easy to hurt **yourself** on a large waterslide.

AVOID THE *Error*

Usually, *you* is not acceptable in formal writing, such as essays for school. *One* is too formal for essays or business letters. In these types of writing, avoid using *you* and *one* by paraphrasing.

✗ **You** need to be careful going out late at night. (too informal for essay)	✓ **People** need to be careful going out late at night.
✗ It's easy to hurt **yourself** on a large waterslide. (too informal for essays)	✓ It's easy **to get hurt** on a large waterslide.
✗ It's easy to hurt **oneself** on a large waterslide. (too formal for most essays or business letters)	

For information on possessive pronouns, see page 111. For demonstrative pronouns, see page 97.

Subject Pronouns

Here are all the subject pronouns:

I	am hungry.
You	are hungry.
He	is hungry.
She	is hungry.
It	is hungry.
We	are hungry.
They	are hungry.

Subject pronouns refer to another noun or person in the situation who is the subject of the sentence.

He lives here.
I am a construction worker.

We use *it* to form impersonal expressions. In impersonal expressions, *it* is not a pronoun and does not replace or refer to another word.

It's raining. **It's** ten o'clock.

For information on expressions with the impersonal *it*, see page 265.

Some languages have only one pronoun for singular nouns. English has three separate pronouns for singular nouns:

he	male
she	female
it	object

AVOID THE *Error*

Do not change pronouns when referring to the same person.

✘ I talked to Luke. **He** told me that **she**'s happy in his new home. **She** lives in an apartment on the third floor. **It** says **he** has a great view of the city from the living room window.

✔ I talked to Luke. **He** told me that **he**'s happy in his new home. **He** lives in an apartment on the third floor. **He** says **he** has a great view of the city from the living room window.

In addition to gender (*he*, *she*, or *it*), English pronouns have number (singular or plural). *He*, *she*, and *it* are singular. *They* is plural.

AVOID THE *Error*

Subject pronouns should agree in gender with the words they replace.

✘ Anne works in this office. **He** is a very hard worker.

✔ Anne works in this office. **She** is a very hard worker.

Subject pronouns should agree in number with the words they replace.

✘ I bought some apples at the market. **It** cost $2 a pound.

✔ I bought some apples at the market. **They** cost $2 a pound.

Use *it* and *they* to refer to people and animals. Use *he* and *she* to refer to people.

AVOID THE *Error*

Do not use *he* and *she* to refer to objects or things. It's possible to use *he* and *she* to refer to animals, especially pets. (Many people say *he* or *she* to refer to pets.)

✘ I love Paris. **She** is a very beautiful city.

✔ I love Paris. **It** is a very beautiful city.

✔ I love my pet cat Irene. **She** is a long-haired Persian.

We use object pronouns after the verb *be.*

It was **me** who spilled coffee all over the break room floor.

AVOID THE *Error*

English speakers no longer use subject pronouns after the verb *be,* though some very traditional grammar books may tell you differently.

✘ It was **I** who spilled coffee all over the break room floor.

✔ It was **me** who spilled coffee all over the break room floor.

A subject is required in all English sentences.

AVOID THE *Error*

Do not omit the subject of an English sentence.

✘ **John** loves fresh fruit. Loves pizza, too.

✔ **John** loves fresh fruit. **He** loves pizza, too.

Compound Subjects

A compound subject consists of two or more nouns or pronouns.

Phil and Erica are getting married next year.
He and she met each other three years ago.

AVOID THE *Error*

For the sake of politeness, people usually mention themselves last in a compound subject.

✘ **I** and **Allen** cleaned the kitchen and bathroom this morning.

✔ **Allen** and **I** cleaned the kitchen and bathroom this morning.

AVOID THE *Error*

Do not use object pronouns in compound subjects.

✘ Byron and **me** are going to the movies tonight.

✔ Byron and **I** are going to the movies tonight.

✘ **Me** and Byron are going to the movies tonight.

Subject Pronouns with *Than* and *As*

In comparative sentences with *than* and *as*, use a subject pronoun when the pronoun is the subject of the comparison.

He is nicer than **she**.
He is as nice as **she**.

AVOID THE *Error*

In informal speech and writing, native speakers often use an object pronoun after *than* and *as*. This is acceptable in everyday speech, but should be avoided in more formal kinds of writing, such as papers for school.

- Formal English

✘ He is nicer than **her**.

✔ He is nicer than **she**.

- Informal English

✔ He is nicer than **her**.

Object Pronouns

Object pronouns receive the action of the verb.

He knows **me.**
He knows **you.**
He knows **him.**
He knows **her.**
He knows **it.**
He knows **us.**
He knows **them.**

Object pronouns can also be the object of a preposition.

The salad is near **me.**
The salad is near **you.**
The salad is near **him.**
The salad is near **her.**
The salad is near **it.**
The salad is near **us.**
The salad is near **them.**

Indirect Objects

An indirect object tells who or what the action was done for. We can express an indirect object in two ways:

- *For* or *to* and the indirect object or pronoun

  Sam moved to Chicago last month, so we gave a going-away party **for him.**

  We gave presents **to them.**

- The verb followed by the indirect and direct objects

  Sam moved to Chicago last month, so we gave **him** a going-away party.

  We gave **them** presents.

With some verbs, we state the indirect object with *for* or *to.* Usually, the preposition *for* implies that someone is being helped.

We sent it **to** them. (They received it.)
We sent it **for** them. (We helped them by mailing it.)
I wrote a letter **for** him. (I helped by writing the letter.)
I wrote a letter **to** him. (I sent him the letter.)

Compound Objects

A compound object consists of two or more nouns or pronouns.

He gave **Mary and him** a thoughtful wedding gift.

For the sake of politeness, people usually mention themselves last in a compound object.

The boss gave Vickie and **me** a difficult assignment.

AVOID THE *Error*

Do not use subject pronouns in compound objects.

✘ Please bring John and **I** some water.	✔ Please bring John and **me** some water.

Indefinite Pronouns

English has a number of indefinite pronouns, such as *all*, *neither*, *several*, *everybody*, *oneself*, *both*, and so on.

Everyone loves ice cream!
Do you want chocolate or vanilla? I don't want **either**. I want strawberry.

Some indefinite pronouns are singular; others are plural.

Singular: another, anybody, anyone, anything, each, either, everybody, everything, nobody, no one, neither, nothing, one, oneself, somebody, someone, something
Plural: both, few, many, others, several

A few indefinite pronouns are singular or plural, depending on the use: *all*, *any*, *more*, *most*, *none*, *some*.

All the neighbors are invited to the block party. (*Neighbors* is plural.)
All the furniture was covered in dust. (*Furniture* is an uncountable noun.)

English speakers use *you* and *they* to make general statements.

You should always stop completely at a red light.
I wonder if the train is late. I hope **they** make an announcement.

English speakers often use *they* and *them* in place of *he* or *she* when they do not know if the person is male or female.

Who's knocking at the door? I don't know, but don't let **them** in.
If an employee loses their ID badge, **they** have to go to the security office to request a new one.

AVOID THE *Error*

In very formal writing, avoid using *they*, *their*, and *them* to refer to unknown or indefinite singular nouns. Use *he* or *she*, or rewrite the sentence.

✘ If an employee loses **their** ID badge, **they** have to go to the security office to request a new one.

✔ If an employee loses **his or her** ID badge, **he or she** has to go to the security office to request a new one.

We can use *it* to refer to conditions in general. This *it* is impersonal and does not refer to a specific noun.

I like **it** here.

Reflexive Pronouns

A reflexive pronoun is an object pronoun that refers to the same person as the subject of the verb. A reflexive pronoun can be a direct or indirect object.

He cut **himself**.
I bought **myself** a new car.

AVOID THE *Error*

You may hear some people use the improper forms *hisself*, *themself*, and *theirselves*. The correct forms are *himself* and *themselves*.

✘ He cut **hisself.**

✔ He cut **himself.**

The reflexive pronouns are the only pronouns in English that have singular and plural forms for *you*: *yourself* and *yourselves.*

Laura, did you hurt **yourself** when you slipped?
You kids need to stop running around, or you'll hurt **yourselves**.

AVOID THE *Error*

Do not use *yourself* or *yourselfs* in place of *yourselves.*

✘ You guys might hurt **yourselfs** if you jump off the train before it stops.

✘ You guys might hurt **yourself** if you jump off the train before it stops.

✔ You guys might hurt **yourselves** if you jump off the train before it stops.

English speakers use reflexive pronouns to emphasize that they are doing the action. In these cases, the word is not a true reflexive.

I cleaned the whole house **myself**.
Mary Lou knitted this sweater **herself**.

AVOID THE *Error*

Avoid pronoun shift. Pronoun shift happens when you refer to a noun with pronouns of a different person, number, or gender. For example, you first refer to a noun with one pronoun, such as *you*, and then switch to another form, such as *they*. When you refer to a noun with a pronoun, all of the pronouns that refer to that noun should be in the same person, gender, and number.

✘ If you practice a sport like roller-skating, it's easy to hurt **oneself** if you're not careful.

✔ If you practice a sport like roller-skating, it's easy to hurt **yourself** if you're not careful.

Reflexive verbs often use reflexive pronouns. Common reflexive verbs include *cut*, *hurt*, *look at*, and *admire*. For more information on reflexive verbs, see page 203.

AVOID THE *Error*

In English, reflexive pronouns are used less frequently than in many other languages.

✗ He **washed himself** before leaving work.	✓ He **washed up** before leaving work.

In English, it's unusual to have a reflexive pronoun and a direct object, unlike other languages.

✗ He washed **himself his hands**.	✓ He washed **his hands**.

Demonstrative Pronouns

This, *that*, *these*, and *those* can be used as pronouns. *This* and *that* are singular; *these* and *those* are plural. Use *this* and *these* for nearby objects or people; use *that* and *those* for distant objects or people.

	NEAR	FAR
Singular	this	that
Plural	these	those

This is delicious.
That is the reason why.
Please give me one of **those**.
I don't like **these**.

AVOID THE *Error*

Avoid unclear reference with pronouns. Unclear reference happens when a pronoun can refer to more than one word or has no clear reference.

✗ Laura told Crystal that **she** looks great today. (*She* can refer to Laura or Crystal.)	✓ Laura told Crystal, "You look great today."
✗ When Mark put the new disk drive in the computer, he broke **it**. (*It* can refer to the disk drive or computer.)	✓ When Mark put the new disk drive in the computer, he broke **the computer**.

Interrogative Pronouns

We use the interrogative pronouns to form questions. The main interrogative pronouns include *who, what, where, when, why,* and *how.*

Who did you call?
What did you order?
Where did you go on vacation?
When did you arrive?
Why did you sell your car?
How did you know?

Exercises

A *Rewrite the sentences by replacing the crossed-out words with a pronoun.*

1. Please tell ~~Mrs. Lynch~~ to come to my office.

2. ~~Mr. and Mrs. Reynolds~~ live in this house.

3. Please put ~~the clean coffee cups~~ in the cupboard.

4. ~~Jennie~~ is a really good teacher.

5. These photocopies are for ~~Mary and Elizabeth~~.

6. I opened ~~the letter~~ at once.

7. ~~You and I~~ need to work as a team to get this work done on time.

8. ~~Mr. Williams~~ is the manager of this office.

B *Complete the sentences by writing* for *or* to.

1. I made some coffee ______________ her.
2. John, I need to talk ______________ you.
3. My father bought a new car ______________ me.
4. You should always tell the truth ______________ a judge.
5. Let's buy a birthday cake ______________ her.

C *Read the sentences. There is one pronoun error in each sentence. Rewrite the sentences, correcting the errors.*

1. Me and Larry are going to Las Vegas next month.

 ____

2. Everyone are here.

 ____

3. Her is one of my best friends.

 ____

4. New York is a huge, busy city. He's a fascinating place to live.

 ____

5. Jonathan and I hurt myself at work yesterday.

 ____

ADJECTIVES

An adjective is a word that modifies, or describes, a noun or a pronoun. Adjectives usually come before the noun.

The clouds are **heavy** and **dark**.

For information on nouns, see page 47.

AVOID THE *Error*

In general, adjectives do not appear after nouns in English.

✘ I'd like some **licorice red**. ✔ I'd like some **red licorice**.

In a few cases, however, adjectives appear after the noun. Adjectives go after:

- Indefinite words

  Let's go **someplace warm**.

- Measurement words

  The pool is **six feet deep**.

- Direct objects

  She painted her car **purple**.

- Linking verbs

  She is **busy** in the kitchen.

For more information on linking verbs, see page 121.

AVOID THE *Error*

Some adjectives do not appear before a noun. They appear only after a linking verb. These verbs include *afraid*, *alive*, *alone*, *asleep*, *ready*, *sorry*, *sure*, and *unable*.

✘ Don't wake up the **asleep** baby.

✔ The baby is **asleep** in the other room.

Common linking verbs include *be*, *become*, *appear*, *smell*, *taste*, and *look*. *Smell*, *taste*, and *look* can be action verbs or linking verbs.

He **tasted** the ice cream. (action verb)
The ice cream **tasted** delicious. (linking verb)

AVOID THE *Error*

Use an adjective, not an adverb, after verbs such as *feel*, *taste*, and *smell*, when they are linking verbs.

✘ I feel **badly**.

✔ I feel **bad**.

For more information on adverbs, see page 221.

Formation of Adjectives

We can use a number of suffixes to form adjectives from verbs and nouns. The following table shows some of these suffixes and the adjectives they form:

SUFFIX	ADJECTIVE
-able/-ible	ador**able**, vis**ible**
-ful	beauti**ful**, wonder**ful**
-ous	humor**ous**
-y	funn**y**
-ly	friend**ly**, neighbor**ly**
-ic	democrat**ic**
-ive	attract**ive**, attent**ive**

AVOID THE *Error*

Adjectives do not have plural forms in English.

✗ We visited three differents cities during our vacation.

✔ We visited three different cities during our vacation.

-ed and *-ing* Adjectives

A number of adjective pairs are formed by adding *-ed* or *-ing* to a verb.

fascinat**ing**	fascinat**ed**
interest**ing**	interest**ed**
stimulat**ing**	stimulat**ed**

Each adjective in the pair has a different meaning. Adjectives ending in *-ing* describe the feeling produced by an object or person. Words ending in *-ed* describe the feelings of a person.

This class is **interesting**.	All the students are **interested** in this class.
I hate this **boring** movie.	I was **bored** during the entire movie.

AVOID THE *Error*

Not all adjectives that end in *-ed* are formed from verbs. Some are formed from nouns. These adjectives do not have *-ing* forms.

✗ Cleveland is a **skill** carpenter and electrician.

✗ Cleveland is a **skilling** carpenter and electrician.

✔ Cleveland is a **skilled** carpenter and electrician.

✗ Her daughter is in a special math class for **gift** children.

✗ Her daughter is in a special math class for **gifting** children.

✔ Her daughter is in a special math class for **gifted** children.

Nouns as Modifiers

Sometimes, a noun can modify another noun.

beef hamburgers   **silk** scarf   **diamond** ring

AVOID THE *Error*

When a noun modifies another noun, the first noun is usually singular.

✗ bees hive   ✓ bee hive

✗ ants colony   ✓ ant colony

If a noun is usually plural or refers to people, it can be plural when modifying another noun.

✗ sport drink   ✓ sports drink

✗ sport car   ✓ sports car

✗ woman golfers   ✓ women golfers

Order of Adjectives

When more than one adjective comes before a noun, the adjectives often are ordered according to the following table:

QUALITY	PHYSICAL DESCRIPTION				ORIGIN	MATERIAL	NOUN
	SIZE	SHAPE	AGE	COLOR			
beautiful			ancient	green	Chinese	porcelain	vase
delicious			fresh		Italian		noodles
interesting	short						story
valuable	large	oval		white			diamond
tall		thin	old		foreign		teacher
sleek			new	red	French		van
hideous				yellow		plastic	flowers
large			new			neoprene	bottle

If the noun has a purpose (a word that says what the noun is used for or used to do), the adjective that describes the purpose goes right before the noun.

a beautiful **flower** vase
a red **delivery** van
a large neoprene **water** bottle
a small plastic **drinking** bottle

Put possessive nouns, possessive adjectives, determiners, and numbers before the first adjective.

Mike's brand-new SUV looks great.
He took **several** beautiful photographs of the parade.
I'd like **four** fresh loaves of Italian whole wheat bread, please.
Mack wants to see **an** exciting action movie, but Sienna wants to see **a** romantic love story.

AVOID THE *Error*

When adjectives come after a linking verb, we usually put ***and*** before the last adjective.

✘	✔
✘ Judy is **blond, beautiful**.	✔ Judy is blond **and** beautiful.
✘ The juice is **cool, refreshing**.	✔ The juice is cool **and** refreshing.

When adjectives come before a noun, we usually leave out ***and***.

✘	✔
✘ A short **and** bossy clerk checked the forms for accuracy.	✔ A **short, bossy** clerk checked the forms for accuracy.
✘ A smart **and** hardworking student will usually get good grades.	✔ A **smart, hardworking** student will usually get good grades.

For information on using commas with adjectives, see page 36.

An intensifier such as *really* or *very* can come before an adjective or group of adjectives.

This chocolate cake is **really** delicious.
He bought a **very** expensive new imported bicycle last year.

An intensifier is a kind of adverb. For information on adverbs, see page 221.

Comparison of Adjectives

We use comparatives and superlatives to compare two or more things. We can talk about which person or thing is bigger, smaller, taller, older, more expensive, and so on. Comparatives are formed with . . . *-er than* and *more . . . than*. We use comparatives to talk about two things. Superlatives are formed with *the . . . -est* and *the most . . . .* We use superlatives to talk about three or more things.

This new bicycle is **cheap**.
That new bicycle is **cheaper**.
This used bicycle is **the cheapest**.

This used car is **expensive**.
The new car is **more expensive**.
That sports car is **the most expensive**.

AVOID THE Error

Do not use the comparative to compare three or more things; use the superlative.

✘ China is the **more** populous country in the world.

✔ China is the **most** populous country in the world.

. . . -er Than and *the . . . -Est*

Use *. . . -er than* and *the . . . -est* with one-syllable adjectives and two-syllable adjectives that end in *-y*.

Chicago's John Hancock Center is **taller than** New York's Empire State Building.
Taipei 101 is **the tallest** building in the world.
This box is **heavier than** that box.
The red box is **the heaviest**.

AVOID THE Error

Do not say *taller from*. Use *taller than*.

✘ John is taller **from** Mike.

✔ John is taller **than** Mike.

To spell comparatives with *-er* and *-est,* follow these rules:

- Add *-er* or *-est* to most adjectives.

hard harder hardest

- When an adjective ends in a consonant + *y*, change the *y* to *i* and add *-er* or *-est*.

heavy	heav**ier**	heav**iest**

- When an adjective ends in a vowel + consonant, double the final consonant and add *-er* or *-est*.

fat	fat**ter**	fat**test**

- When an adjective ends in a vowel, add *-r* or *-st*.

nice	nice**r**	nice**st**

More . . . Than and *The Most . . .*

Use *more . . . than* and *the most . . .* with most adjectives of two or more syllables.

Kelly is **more beautiful than** Melissa. Kelly is **the most beautiful** girl in school.

English is **more difficult than** Spanish. Arabic is **the most difficult** language.

AVOID THE *Error*

A few two-syllable adjectives use *-er*: *simple*, *quiet*, *narrow*, and *shallow*.

✘ The other end of the pool is **more shallow** than this one.

✔ The other end of the pool is **shallower** than this one.

A few adjectives have two forms, such as *handsome* and *angry*.

Joel is **more handsome than** Conroy.

Joel is **handsomer than** Conroy.

AVOID THE *Error*

Avoid double comparatives and superlatives.

✘ Ms. Lin is the **most** nicest teacher at our school.

✔ Ms. Lin is **the nicest** teacher at our school.

Irregular Comparatives and Superlatives

Some adjectives do not follow the regular pattern. The following table shows some important irregular comparatives and superlatives:

ADJECTIVE	COMPARATIVE	SUPERLATIVE
good	better	best
bad	worse	worst

AVOID THE *Error*

Do not use *more good* for *better* or *the most good* for *the best.*

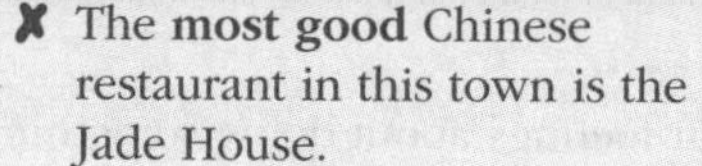

✘ The **most good** Chinese restaurant in this town is the Jade House.

✔ The **best** Chinese restaurant in this town is the Jade House.

Here are some sentences with examples of adjectives that do not follow the regular pattern.

His grades this year are much **worse than** last year's.
He wore his **best** suit to the party.

AVOID THE *Error*

Do not use *best* in place of an adjective such as *great, excellent,* or another positive adjective. Use *best* only when you are comparing three or more things.

✘ I hope you have a **best** vacation.

✔ I hope you have a **great** vacation.

When the comparison is equal, we use *as . . . as . . . .*

John is **as** nice **as** Mary.

Expressions with *So* + Adjective + *That*

We can use *so* + adjective + *that* to talk about extreme conditions and their consequences.

She is **so intelligent that** she graduated from high school when she was sixteen.
I'm **so tired that** I need to take a nap.

Expressions with *Too . . . To*

Too . . . to can be used to talk about extreme conditions and their consequences.

I am **too** tired **to** work.
John's son is still **too** young **to** talk.

We can say *too* + adjective in shortened versions of *too . . . to* expressions, especially in informal settings.

It's **too** hot. (meaning that it's too hot to be comfortable, to do anything, etc.)

Expressions with *So . . . To . . .*

So . . . to can be used to describe our feelings about doing something.

I am **so** excited **to** meet her.
I am **so** happy **to** have passed that test.

We can also use *so* + adjective to express a strong feeling. This is especially common in informal language. Usually speakers say *so* with special emphasis.

This yogurt is **so** good!
Allen is **so** cute!

AVOID THE *Error*

Be careful about substituting *too* for *very*, *so*, or *really*. Sometimes doing so changes the meaning.

He is **very** proud to meet her. (He is extremely proud.)

He is **too** proud to meet her. (Because of his pride, he won't meet her.)

Sometimes, the substitution does not make sense.

✔ I am **very** happy to meet you. ✘ I am **too** happy to meet you.

Adjectives + Infinitives and Adjectives + *That* Clauses

These adjectives can be followed with an infinitive or a *that* clause to tell how someone feels about a situation:

afraid	proud	sad	happy
surprised	delighted	sorry	unhappy

Use a *that* clause if the subjects are different.

I am happy **that you came.**
I was surprised **that we won.**

Use a *that* clause or an infinitive if the subjects are the same.

I am happy **to come.**	I am happy **that I came.**
I am happy **to be here.**	I am happy **that I am here.**

These adjectives are often used with an infinitive that gives more information:

able ready likely

We are ready **to leave.**
I'm sorry. I'm not able **to go** to your party.

Exercises

A *Write the words in parentheses in the correct order. Use commas as necessary.*

1. Let's order some (**warm/garlic/nice**) bread to eat with the spaghetti.

 ____

2. (**green/favorite/cotton/John's**) T-shirt is lying on the floor.

 ____

3. Those (**rain/dark/heavy**) clouds make me think a thunderstorm is coming.

 ____

4. She bought a (**yellow/hybrid/new**) car this year.

 ____

5. She bought an (**expensive/Chinese/antique**) teapot.

 ____

B *Using the word in parentheses, complete the sentences by writing an adjective with -ed or -ing on the line.*

1. This book is really ____________ (**interest**).
2. I felt ____________ (**bore**) during Professor Smith's class.
3. We were ____________ (**excite**) to receive your letter.
4. Jean felt ____________ (**frighten**), so she locked the front door.
5. Working in a factory can be a ____________ (**bore**) job.

C *Write the comparative or superlative form of the adjective in parentheses. Use* . . . -er than, the . . . -est, more . . . than, *or* the most . . . .

1. The Mississippi is ____________ (**long**) river in the United States.
2. The diving pool is ____________ (**deep**) the swimming pool.
3. A Lexus is ____________ (**expensive**) a Volkswagen.
4. I think that Kelly is ____________ (**good**) player on the team.
5. This is the ____________ (**delicious**) soup I've ever tried.
6. I think that yellow roses are ____________ (**beautiful**) red roses.
7. The anaconda is one of ____________ (**dangerous**) snakes in the world.
8. Today is ____________ (**warm**) yesterday.
9. This is the ____________ (**boring**) movie I've ever seen.
10. John's test score is ____________ (**high**) Frank's.

POSSESSIVE WORDS

Possessive words show who owns something. These words also show who or what something belongs to. We use possessive words in place of possessive nouns. There are two kinds of possessives: possessive adjectives and possessive pronouns. For information on possessive nouns, see page 54.

We use possessive adjectives in front of nouns. The possessive adjective shows who or what the noun belongs to.

His computer isn't working today.
Marianne parked **her** car down the street.

We use possessive pronouns in place of nouns. A possessive pronoun can be the subject of a sentence, be the object, or follow a verb such as *be*.

My coat is blue. (subject)	**Mine** is blue.
Please help her find **her coat**. (object)	Please help me find **hers**.
Those coats are **Chuck's and Nancy's**. (follows *be*)	Those coats are **theirs**.

AVOID THE *Error*

Do not use apostrophes with possessive adjectives or pronouns.

✘ I think that he lost **his'** pens.	✔ I think that he lost **his** pens.
✘ I think that these packages are **our's**.	✔ I think that these packages are **ours.**

This table shows all the possessive adjectives and possessive pronouns:

POSSESSIVE ADJECTIVE	POSSESSIVE PRONOUN
my	mine
your	yours
his	his
her	hers
its	—
our	ours
their	theirs

AVOID THE Error

Do not use *the* + possessive adjective. Use *the* or the possessive adjective.

✘ Look at **the her** new car. ✔ Look at **her** new car.

✔ Look at **the** new car.

Do not use *the* + possessive pronoun. Use only the possessive pronoun.

✘ That new car is **the hers**. ✔ That new car is **hers**.

Your and *yours* are both singular and plural.

John, I love **your** new hat.
John and Mary, I love **your** new car.

John, is this hat **yours**?
John and Mary, is that new car **yours**?

AVOID THE Error

There is no possessive pronoun *its*.

✘ That water bowl is **its**. ✔ That water bowl is **the dog's**.

His and *her* agree with the possessor.

I heard that Mary has a new boyfriend. **Her** new boyfriend is really cute!

AVOID THE *Error*

His and *her* should agree with the possessor, not with the thing possessed.

✘ I heard that Mary has a new boyfriend. **His** new boyfriend is really cute!

✔ I heard that Mary has a new boyfriend. **Her** new boyfriend is really cute!

His is both a possessive pronoun and a possessive adjective.

His name is Max. (possessive adjective)
That car is **his**. (possessive pronoun)

AVOID THE *Error*

Mines is not a possessive pronoun. The correct word is *mine*.

✘ These DVDs are **mines**.

✔ These DVDs are **mine**.

In many languages, speakers use possessive adjectives less frequently than English speakers do. English tends to use these words where other languages use *the*.

AVOID THE *Error*

With objects that are closely associated with us, such as clothing or possessions, use a possessive adjective, not *the*.

✘ I need to put on **the** shoes.

✔ I need to put on **my** shoes.

✘ He took off **the** hat.

✔ He took off **his** hat.

Use possessive adjectives to talk about parts of our bodies.

I need to wash **my** hands.
I hurt **my** knee while I was rock climbing.

AVOID THE *Error*

Do not use *the* to talk about body parts. Use a possessive adjective.

✘ Please wash **the** hands before dinner.	✔ Please wash **your** hands before dinner.

However, if another part of the sentence makes the owner of the body part clear, use *the*.

✘ I hit myself in **my** head.	✔ I hit myself in **the** head.

In English, we use possessive adjectives to talk about our serving of food.

I'd like some ice cream with **my** pie, please.

AVOID THE *Error*

Do not confuse the possessive adjective:

- *Their* with *there* or *they're*

✘ Please tell the guests to leave **they're** hats and coats in the bedroom.	✔ Please tell the guests to leave **their** hats and coats in the bedroom.
✘ Please tell the guests to leave **there** hats and coats in the bedroom.	

- *Its* with the contraction *it's* (*it is*)

✘ The dog is thirsty. Please put some water in **it's** bowl.	✔ The dog is thirsty. Please put some water in **its** bowl.

- *Your* with the contraction *you're* (*you are*)

✘ **You're** cooking is delicious, Jennifer.	✔ **Your** cooking is delicious, Jennifer.

Possessive adjectives and possessive pronouns should agree with the words they replace.

This book is **Mary's**.	This book is **hers**.
You had a good idea.	**Your** idea is a good one.

AVOID THE *Error*

Avoid pronoun shift.

✗ If **you** leave your apartment, make sure you lock **their** doors.	✓ If **you** leave your apartment, make sure you lock **your** doors.

When a noun has adjectives before it, the possessive adjective goes before the adjectives.

What is **your** favorite food?
I lost my **new** green pen.

AVOID THE *Error*

Do not use *the* before a possessive adjective or pronoun.

✗ That computer is **the** hers.	✓ That computer is hers.
✗ This is **the** her office.	✓ This is her office.

We can use possessive pronouns in expressions with *of.*

Raymond is a good friend **of mine**.
Do you know Ron Pope? A friend **of his** can get us tickets to the big basketball game!

AVOID THE *Error*

Avoid unclear references with pronouns. An unclear reference happens when a pronoun can refer to more than one word or has no clear reference.

✘ Laura told Ellen that she found **her** book. (*Her* can refer to either *Laura* or *Ellen*.)

✔ Laura told Ellen, "I found my book."

We can use *own* and *of (my) own* to emphasize possessive adjectives.

I have my **own** car now. I just bought a new convertible!

I have a car **of my own**. I am no longer using my parent's car.

AVOID THE *Error*

Avoid overusing *own*. Use *own* only when necessary to clarify that something belongs to oneself and not another person, or is separate from another's.

✘ Type your answers on your own keyboard. (*Own* is not necessary; it's implied you will use your keyboard.)

✔ Type your answers on your keyboard.

✔ Write your answers on your **own** paper. (Do not write on another's paper, or do not write in the book but rather on other paper.)

✔ Write your answers on **your paper**. (Write your answers on the paper you have.)

Own is also a verb.

John **owns** that apartment building.

AVOID THE *Error*

Do not use possessive pronouns with *own*. Use possessive adjectives.

✗ She has a car of **hers** own. ✓ She has a car of **her** own.

We can form possessives with a phrase with *of* and a possessive pronoun.

I saw a good friend **of mine** yesterday.

AVOID THE *Error*

Use a possessive pronoun, not a possessive adjective, after *of*.

✗ I met some friends of **him** at the meeting. ✓ I met some friends of **his** at the meeting.

We use *whose* to ask questions about who owns something. The answer to a question with *whose* is a possessive word.

Whose book is this? It's **mine**.
Whose is this? It's **hers**.

AVOID THE *Error*

Do not confuse *who's* and *whose*. *Who's* is the abbreviation for *who is*.

✗ **Whose** on first base? ✓ **Who's** on first base?

✗ **Who's** book is this? ✓ **Whose** book is this?

Exercises

A *Complete the sentences by circling the correct word.*

1. This book is (**my/mine**).
2. It's a shame that he wrecked (**her/hers**) car in the accident.
3. (**They're/Their/There**) vacation begins next Thursday.
4. Which car is (**their/theirs**)?
5. John, please don't leave (**your/you're/yours**) shoes in the middle of the living room floor.
6. Which desks are (**our/ours**)?
7. This jacket is (**him/his**).
8. She bought (**her/hers**) house in 2006.
9. You can play games using the mouse and screen on (**your/yours/you're**) computer.
10. Listen! (**My/Mine**) favorite song is playing on the radio.

B *Complete the sentences with a possessive adjective or pronoun by giving the correct form of the word in parentheses, following the example.*

1. I think that this pen is ______________. (I)
2. Where did you put ______________ coat? (you)
3. We need to be more careful with ______________ money. (us)
4. Our neighbor always parks ______________ car in front of our house. (he)
5. Be careful with those antique plates. They're not ______________. (you)
6. Mr. and Mrs. Benny are very careful with ______________ money. (they)
7. Make sure you lock ______________ apartment door at night. (you)
8. The airline lost ______________ luggage, so I had to buy new clothes during my vacation. (I)
9. This isn't my notebook. ______________ is dark red. (I)
10. My birthday is July 15. When is ______________? (you)

VERBS

Verbs are words that indicate an action or a state.

He **is running**. (action)
He **feels** tired. (state)

A sentence can have a single verb or a verb phrase.

Rabbits **love** carrots.
The rabbit **is eating** a carrot now.

A verb phrase is formed with an auxiliary verb (*be* or *have*) plus a present or past participle.

He **is eating** now.
He **has eaten** dinner already.

For information on present participles, see page 136. For information on past participles, see page 161–163.

A verb phrase can also be formed with a modal verb and a verb.

He **will** arrive soon.
He **might** bring a present.

For information on modal verbs, see page 174.

Verb Tense

Verbs change forms to show different tenses. A tense tells when the action happened.

She **loves** her new home. (present)
He **shopped** at the supermarket yesterday. (past)
They **will arrive** tomorrow. (future)

Verb forms also show whether the action is always true, completed, or in progress.

Giraffes **have** long necks. (always true)
She **is running**. (in progress)
He's been a teacher for three years. (began in the past and is true now)

Many verbs are related to nouns or adjectives and have the same forms.

We **raced** each other. She won the **race**.
The room is **clean**. Let's **clean** the room.
They put the juice in **bottles**. They **bottled** the juice.

Sometimes, a suffix will change a word into a verb.

He lowered the shades to dark**en** the room..
He will author**ize** the employees to leave early.

This table shows suffixes that can change words to verbs:

SUFFIX	FUNCTION	WORD	VERB
-fy	changes a noun to a verb	glory	glori**fy**
-ize	changes a noun to a verb	author	author**ize**
-en	changes an adjective to a verb	dark	dark**en**
-ate	changes an adjective to a verb	active	activ**ate**

AVOID THE *Error*

Do not make new verbs from nouns or adjectives.

✘ She **colded** the juice. ✔ She **chilled** the juice.

✘ The mechanic **lubrified** the car. ✔ The mechanic **lubricated** the car.

Transitive and Intransitive Verbs

Verbs can be transitive or intransitive. Transitive and intransitive verbs are all action verbs—they show actions. Transitive verbs can have a direct object.

He ate **an apple**.

An intransitive verb **cannot** have a direct object.

He **swims** every morning.

AVOID THE *Error*

Do not use a direct object with an intransitive verb.

✗ He swam **her**. ✓ He swam.

✓ He swam **with her**.

In the last sentence, ***with her*** is a prepositional phrase that modifies the verb. It is not a direct object.

Linking Verbs

A linking verb connects the subject of a sentence to information about the subject. Linking verbs are not action verbs. Linking verbs show a state. Common linking verbs include *be*, *become*, and *seem*.

Rhonda **is** a teacher.
Marylou **is** sick today.
Jane **became** a teacher in 2007.
Mark **seems** tired today.

A linking verb can be followed by an adjective, adverb, or noun.

The book **is expensive**. (adjective)
The book is **on the table**. (prepositional phrase that functions as an adverb)
The book is **a masterpiece**. (noun)

A noun can follow a verb such as *be* or *become*, but these nouns are not direct objects. These nouns are complements of verbs. A complement refers to the subject of the sentence.

He became **a teacher** in 2008. (*Teacher* refers to *he*.)
She is our **neighbor**. (*Neighbor* refers to *her*.)

AVOID THE *Error*

Even though complements are not objects of the verb, speakers normally do not use subject pronouns for them. They use object pronouns.

Who's at the door? ✗ It's **I**, Tim. ✓ It's **me**, Tim.

For more information about pronouns, see page 88.

Some verbs, such as *feel*, *taste*, *smell*, *look*, and *turn*, can be linking verbs or action verbs with different but related meanings. This table shows related linking and action verbs:

LINKING VERB	ACTION VERB
This cheese **tastes** terrible.	Tim **tasted** the cheese.
Magda **turned** red.	Magda **turned** the page.
You **look** tired.	Please **look** at page 21.
She **appears** tired.	Harry Potter suddenly **appeared** out of nowhere.

The following chapters will give more detail on each verb tense.

VERBS
Be: Simple Present Tense

We use the present tense of *be* to show a state or a quality of something at present.

I **am** happy to meet you.
He'**s** very sleepy this morning.
She **is** sick today.
The sky **is** gray today.
Are you ready to order?
They'**re** very busy today.

We also use the present tense of *be* to show a state or quality that is always true.

The sky **is** blue.
Marge **is** a very nice person.

We can follow the verb *be* with a noun, an adjective, or an adverb.

She's an **engineer**. (noun)
She's **happy** today. (adjective)
He's **in his office**. (prepositional phrase that functions as an adverb)

AVOID THE *Error*

Do not use *have* with adjectives or nouns such as *hot, cold, hunger/hungry,* or *thirst/thirsty.* Use *be* + adjective.

✘ I **have** cold. ✔ I **am** cold.

Do not use *have* to state one's age. Use *be* + the age.

✘ I **have** twenty years. ✔ I **am** twenty years old.

Formation

This table shows the affirmative forms of the verb *be*:

I	**am ('m)**	cold.
He / She / It	**is ('s)**	cold.
We / You / They	**are ('re)**	cold.

AVOID THE Error

Do not use *be* in place of *am*, *is*, *are*, and so on.

✘ He **be** tired.	✔ He **is** tired.

This table shows the negative forms of the simple present tense of *be*:

I	**am not ('m not)**	cold.
He / She / It	**is not ('s not *or* isn't)**	cold.
We / You / They	**are not ('re not *or* aren't)**	cold.

AVOID THE Error

Do not insert *no* into a sentence to make it negative. Use *not* or a contraction of *not*.

✘ Anita is **no** busy.	✔ Anita is **not** busy.
	✔ Anita **isn't** busy.
✘ We are **no** from China.	✔ We are **not** from China.
	✔ We **aren't** from China.
	✔ We're **not** from China.

In everyday speech and writing, we use contractions. In formal writing, avoid contractions.

INFORMAL	FORMAL
He's a teacher	**He is** a teacher.
They're experts in their fields.	**They are** experts in their fields.

AVOID THE *Error*

Do not confuse homonyms such as *its* and *it's*, *we're* and *were*, or *they're*, *their*, and *there*. Pronoun + verb contractions (such as *it's* and *they're)* always have an apostrophe. The possessive *its* never has an apostrophe.

✗ I just got a new dog. **Its** very friendly and good with children.

✔ I just got a new dog. **It's** very friendly and good with children.

✗ **Were** ready to leave.

✔ **We're** ready to leave.

✗ I think that **their** lost.

✗ I think **there** lost.

✔ I think that **they're** lost.

For more information on homonyms, see page 15.

He, *she*, *it*, *we*, *you*, and *they* + *be* + *not* all have two contracted forms. The two forms can be used interchangeably.

They're not here. **They aren't** here.

I am not has only one contracted form: *I'm not.*

I'm not in my car. I'm on the bus.

AVOID THE *Error*

Do not use *amn't* or *ain't.* Use *I am not* or *I'm not.*

✗ I **ain't** late.

✗ I **amn't** late.

✔ I **am not** late.

✔ **I'm not** late.

Forms of *be* can also be in contractions with nouns, proper nouns, and question words in speech and informal writing.

Where'**s** the bathroom?
When'**s** the meeting?
How'**s** the salad?
Pat'**s** the boss.
The door'**s** open. Please close it.

AVOID THE *Error*

In contractions, apostrophes replace the letters that are deleted.

✗ He **is'nt** at work today.	✓ He **isn't** at work today.
✗ **Theyr'e** at the supermarket.	✓ **They're** at the supermarket.

Questions with *Be* in the Simple Present Tense

Yes/No Questions

To form *yes/no* questions (questions that can be answered with either *yes* or *no*), invert the subject and the verb and add a question mark:

She is running for president. → **Is** she running for president?
They are ready to leave. → **Are** they ready to leave?

AVOID THE *Error*

In informal speech and writing, you may indicate a *yes/no* question with rising intonation only (that is, without the inversion of subject and verb) and a question mark—often when expressing surprise. In formal writing, always invert the subject and verb and use a question mark.

✗ **She's** married? I thought she was single! (formal)	✓ **She's** married? I thought she was single! (informal)
✗ Many participants have **signed up** for the workshop? (formal)	✓ **Have** many participants **signed up** for the workshop? (formal)

Wh- Questions

To form *wh-* questions, add a *wh-* word (question word) and invert the subject and verb.

Where's the bathroom?
How's the weather today?

AVOID THE *Error*

When *who* is the subject of a question, the subject and verb are not inverted. *Who* is the first word in the question.

✗ **Is who** ready to leave? ✔ **Who is** ready to leave?

Normally, when speaking, people do not say *am I not* in questions. They usually say *aren't I.*

Why **aren't I** getting a raise?
Aren't I a good student?

AVOID THE *Error*

Do not use *I* + *aren't* in statements.

✗ I **aren't** a teacher. ✔ I'**m not** a teacher.

Exercises

A *Write the contraction on the line.*

1. I am ________
2. he is ________
3. she is ________
4. it is ________
5. you are ________
6. we are ________
7. they are ________

8. they are not ______________
9. it is not ______________
10. we are not ______________

B *Complete the sentences by writing* am, is, *or* are *on the line.*

1. I ________ tired today.
2. She ________ a good student.
3. They ________ very nice neighbors.
4. He ________ at the mall.
5. I think that you ________ wrong about that.
6. You ________ late to work all the time.
7. We ________ ready to leave for the movies.
8. I ________ at work right now.
9. These grapes ________ delicious.
10. Tom and Susan ________ married.

C *Write the affirmative or negative form of* be *on the line.*

1. Carlos is happy today. He ______________ sad.
2. Sally isn't a librarian. She ______________ a teacher.
3. That car is new. It ______________ used.
4. These books ______________ expensive. They're cheap.
5. The children ______________ thirsty. But they're hungry.
6. The house ______________ dirty. It's clean.
7. Potato chips ______________ salty. They aren't sweet.
8. This book isn't boring. It ______________ interesting.
9. The water isn't cold. It ______________ warm.
10. The girls ______________ busy. They're studying for a big test.

VERBS
Simple Present Tense

We use the simple present tense to talk about:

- Things that are always true

  Cats **hate** water.

- Things that happen regularly

  School **starts** in fall.

- Habits and routines

  I always **get up** at 5:00 A.M.

- Future actions that are part of a schedule

  My train **leaves** at 5:21 P.M.

AVOID THE Error

Verbs such as *believe, hate, know, like,* and *love* are never used in the progressive tenses. Use the simple present tense to talk about these actions in the present.

✗ Tom **is knowing** French. ✓ Tom **knows** French.

✗ Rhonda **is really liking** her new apartment. ✓ Rhonda really **likes** her new apartment.

Verbs that are usually *not* used in the progressive tenses include:

believe
feel
forget
hate
have (possess)
know
like
love

mean
need
own
prefer
remember
seem
want

We also use the simple present tense in simple conditional sentences. See page 258 for more information about these sentences. For more information on the present progressive, see page 136. For more information on the past progressive tense, see page 158.

Formation

This table shows the affirmative forms of the simple present tense:

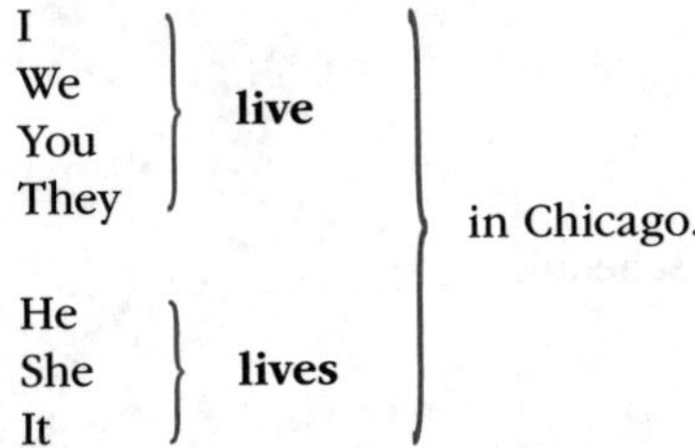

Subject	Verb	
I / We / You / They	**live**	in Chicago.
He / She / It	**lives**	in Chicago.

AVOID THE Error

Don't forget to add *-s* (or *-es*) to the base form of simple present-tense verbs with *he*, *she*, and *it*.

✘ He **like** that restaurant. ✔ He **likes** that restaurant.

Do not add *-s* (or *-es*) to simple present-tense verbs with *I*, *you*, *we*, and *they*.

✘ I **likes** that restaurant. ✔ I **like** that restaurant.

This table shows the negative forms of the simple present tense:

Subject	Auxiliary	
I / We / You / They	**do not (don't)**	live in Chicago.
He / She / It	**does not (doesn't)**	live in Chicago.

AVOID THE *Error*

Do not add *-s* (or *-es*) to the main verb in negative sentences.

✗ I don't **likes** that restaurant. ✓ I don't **like** that restaurant.

Spelling the Simple Present Tense

To spell the *he*, *she*, and *it* forms of simple present tense verbs, follow these rules:

- Add *-s* to the base forms of most verbs.

  learn—learn**s** read—read**s** eat—eat**s** sleep—sleep**s**

- Add *-es* to the base forms of verbs that end in *-s*, *-sh*, *-ch*, *-z*, or *-o*.

  buzz—buzz**es** kiss—kiss**es** miss—miss**es** do—do**es**

- For verbs that end in consonant + *y*, change the *y* to *i* and add *-es* to the verb.

  try—tr**ies** fly—fl**ies** study—stud**ies** reply—repl**ies**

- For verbs that end in vowel + *y*, add *-s*.

  buy—buy**s** stay—stay**s** play—play**s**

- *Have* is irregular: *has*.

  He **has** a brand-new car.

Pronouncing Simple Present-Tense Verbs

To pronounce the *he*, *she*, and *it* forms of simple present-tense verbs, follow these rules:

- With verbs that end in /s, z, ʃ, tʃ/, and /ʤ/, pronounce the ending /əz/.

  kisses buzzes washes teaches fixes judges

- Pronounce the ending as /s/ with verbs that end in a voiceless consonant such as /f, t, k, p/. (The vocal chords do not vibrate when you say voiceless sounds.)

  stops kicks laughs writes

- Pronounce the ending as /z/ with verbs ending in a vowel or a voiced consonant such as /v, d, g, n, m, l/. (The vocal chords vibrate when you say vowels and voiced consonants.)

rides drives smiles mines pays does flies

For more information on voiced and voiceless sounds, see page 4.

Adverbs with the Simple Present Tense

We often use adverbs such as *always*, *sometimes*, *never*, *usually*, and *rarely* with the simple present tense.

He **always** arrives late.
She **never** gets sick.
Sometimes, traffic to the beach is backed up for miles.

AVOID THE *Error*

Do not use the present tense of *use to* to talk about habits in the present. Use the simple present tense. *Use to* is used in the past tense (*used to*).

✘ I **use to** live in Texas. ✔ I live in Texas.

Use *be* + *used to* + gerund to talk about things you are accustomed to.

A gerund is a verb ending in *-ing* that functions as a noun. For more information on gerunds, see page 210.

I **am used to getting up** at 5:00 A.M. every day.

Questions in the Simple Present Tense

To form questions with the simple present tense, we use the auxiliary verb *do*.

Yes/No Questions

For *yes/no* questions, delete the ending from the verb, if any, and add *do* or *does* and a question mark.

He likes action movies. → **Does** he like action movies?
I like broccoli. → **Do** you like broccoli?

AVOID THE *Error*

When you form a question where the main verb is *do*, do not omit the word *do*.

✘ Does he any work? ✔ Does he **do** any work?

✘ Do they well in school? ✔ Do they **do** well in school?

Wh- Questions

To form *wh-* questions, add a question word, delete the ending from the verb (if any), and add a form of *do* and a question mark.

He live**s** in China. → **Where does** he live?

AVOID THE *Error*

Delete *-s* from the main verb in questions in the simple present tense, and add it to *do* (*does*). Do not repeat *-s* (or *-es*) with the main verb in questions.

✘ **Do** she **likes** Italian food? ✔ **Does** she **like** Italian food?

✘ What time **do** the party begin**s**? ✔ What time **does** the party begin?

When the question word is the subject of the question, do not use *do*. Add a question word and a question mark.

Mr. and Mrs. Elliott live in this house.

Who lives in this house?

Exercises

A *Complete the sentences by writing the verb in parentheses in the simple present tense.*

1. Tom ______________ (**live**) in California.
2. Every day, my children ______________ (**play**) in the park.
3. Mrs. Williams ______________ (**leave**) for work at seven o'clock every day.
4. Every day Mary ______________ (**send**) a lot of e-mails to her friends.
5. My manager always ______________ (**check**) my work carefully.
6. Francisco ______________ (**have**) a new car.
7. They ______________ (**work**) at Discount Shoes.
8. Ted never ______________ (**watch**) reality shows on TV.
9. She always ______________ (**study**) English at night, after her children go to sleep.
10. She usually ______________ (**finish**) work at 10:30 at night.

B *Write questions for which the underlined words are the answers, following the example.*

1. He lives in Chicago.
   Where does he live?
2. They usually eat dinner at six o'clock.
   ____
3. Mary works in this office.
   ____
4. David studies English at night.
   ____
5. Christine has two children.
   ____

C *Rewrite the sentences in the negative, using* don't *or* doesn't.

1. Mary likes Italian food.

 ____

2. Frank and Mark drive to work together every day.

 ____

3. Maria watches TV at night after work.

 ____

4. I like to go to the movies on Friday nights.

 ____

5. He studies English at Dyson Community College.

 ____

VERBS
Present Progressive Tense

We use the present progressive tense to talk about:

- Actions that are happening right now

  He's cooking dinner.

- Future plans

  After work **I'm going** to a concert.

Formation

We form the present progressive tense with a form of the verb *be* and a present participle (a verb + *-ing*).

John **is driving** to work.
Bill and Mary **are watching** TV.

AVOID THE Error

Use a complete verb phrase in the present progressive tense. Do not omit the form of the verb *be*.

✗ He driving home. ✓ He **is** driving home.

Do not use the base form *be*.

✗ He **be** driving home. ✓ He **is** driving home.

This table shows the affirmative and negative forms of the present progressive tense:

I	**am ('m)**	**(not)**	
He / She / It	**is ('s)**	**(not/isn't)**	**going** to the store.
We / You / They	**are ('re)**	**(not/aren't)**	

AVOID THE *Error*

Verbs such as *believe*, *hate*, *know*, *like*, and *love* are not normally used in the progressive tenses. Use the simple present tense to talk about them in the present tense.

✗ Tom **is hating** his ex-wife. ✓ Tom **hates** his ex-wife.

✗ Sam **is believing** that the world is flat. ✓ Sam **believes** that the world is flat.

For a list of verbs normally not used in the progressive tenses, see pages 129–130.

Verbs that refer to the senses, such as *taste*, *smell*, and so on, have slightly different meanings in the present progressive and simple present tenses. In the simple present tense, they refer to the feeling or sensation that something causes. In the present progressive tense, they refer to the action of smelling, tasting, and so on.

That cheese **tastes** terrible!
He **is tasting** the cheese.

AVOID THE *Error*

Do not use the simple present tense to talk about an action that is in progress in the present. Use the present progressive.

✗ Watch out! A car **comes**. ✓ Watch out! A car **is coming**.

Spelling Present Participles

A few simple spelling rules help you write present participles correctly.

- Add *-ing* to most base verbs.

eat	eat**ing**
sleep	sleep**ing**
buy	buy**ing**

- If a verb ends in *-ie*, change *-ie* to y and add *-ing*.

die	**dying**

- If a verb ends in a consonant and *-e*, drop the *-e* and add *-ing*.

come	com**ing**
write	writ**ing**
dance	danc**ing**

- If a one-syllable verb ends in a vowel and a consonant, double the consonant and add *-ing*.

run	run**ning**
get	get**ting**
stop	stop**ping**

- If a two-syllable verb is stressed on the last syllable and ends in a vowel and a consonant, double the consonant and add *-ing*.

begin**ning**

AVOID THE *Error*

When adding *-ing*, do not double the final consonant of a two-syllable verb if the first syllable of the verb is stressed.

✘ happen**n**ing	✔ happen**ing**

Questions in the Present Progressive Tense

Yes/No Questions

To form *yes/no* questions in the present progressive tense, invert the subject and the verb *be* (*is/are*) and add a question mark.

He is driving to work today → **Is he** driving to work today?

Wh- Questions

To form *wh-* questions, add a *wh-* word, invert the subject and the verb *be* (*is/are*), and add a question mark.

They are going to work. → **Where are** they going?

AVOID THE Error

If the question word is the subject of the sentence, do not invert the subject and *be*. *Who* is the first word in the question.

✗ **Is who** using the computer? ✓ **Who** is using the computer?

Exercises

A *What are they doing? Write sentences using the present progressive tense and following the example.*

1. Robert/cook/dinner.

   Robert is cooking dinner.

2. Jean/set/the table.

   ______

3. Bob and Larry/watch TV/in the living room.

   ______

4. I/not/talk/on the phone.

   ______

5. We/play/cards after dinner.

   ______

6. David/talk to/a friend in Japan.

____

7. Vickie and Joanne/study/in the library.

____

8. Alan/drive/home.

____

9. We/clean/the bathrooms.

____

10. They/take/the ten o'clock train tomorrow.

____

B *For each sentence, write a matching yes/no question.*

1. Phil and Cathy are exercising in the park.

____

2. Frank is playing computer games.

____

3. I am listening to music.

____

4. The children are playing a game.

____

5. We are having fun.

____

C *Complete the sentences by writing the verb in parentheses in the simple present tense or present progressive tense.*

1. Tom ____________________ (**wash**) his new car every Sunday.
2. Right now, Tom ____________________ (**wash**) his car at the car wash.
3. In summer, Mrs. William ____________________ (**play**) tennis every day after work.
4. Today Mrs. Williams ____________________ (**play**) tennis with her best friend, Betty Mahaffey.

5. My dog usually____________________ (**sleep**) most of the time.
6. Right now, my dog ____________________ (**sleep**) near the fireplace.
7. Pedro and Allen ____________________ (**do**) their English homework every night after dinner.
8. At the moment, they ____________________ (**not study**). They ____________________ (**work**).
9. Tina ____________________ (**talk**) on the phone with her mother now.
10. She ____________________ (**call**) her mother every night at 9:30.
11. We ____________________ (**make**) cookies every year during the holidays.
12. Right now, we ____________________ (**make**) gingerbread cookies.

VERBS
Imperatives

We use imperatives to give commands, make offers or invitations, give directions, and give warnings.

Formation

Form imperatives using the base form of the verb.

Be quiet! (command)
Stop talking! (command)
Have a can of soda! (offer)
Turn left at the fountain. (directions)
Watch out! A bus is coming. (warning)

For negative imperatives, use *do not* or *don't*.

Don't walk on the grass.
Do not drink coffee at bedtime.

Use *let's* to make suggestions and give commands that include the speaker. *Let's* is short for *let us*.

Let's go shopping.
Let's hurry up.

The negative form of *let's* is *let's not*:

Let's not forget our umbrellas today. It looks like rain.

AVOID THE Error

We use exclamation marks with imperatives to express strong emotion. If the imperative is a simple instruction or explanation, an exclamation mark is not needed.

✘ Watch out for the car.	✔ Watch out for the car! (said when a car is about to hit someone)
✘ Turn left at Green Street!	✔ Turn left at Green Street. (said as a simple instruction)

For more information on exclamation marks, see pages 32–33.

We can add *you* to an imperative to soften the imperative or to get the listener's attention.

You sit here for the present.

Making Polite Requests

Imperatives are not always the best way to make a suggestion or a polite request. To make polite requests, you can add the word *please* to an imperative. *Please* can come at the beginning or end of a sentence.

Please hang your coat in the hall closet.
Hang your coat in the hall closet, **please**.

English speakers can also use *let's* to soften the imperative.

Let's hang your coat in the hall closet.

In addition, English speakers can use sentences and questions with modal verbs such as *can* or *could*.

You **can** hang your coat in the closet.
Can you hang your coat in the closet?
Could you hang your coat in the closet?

For information on modal verbs, see page 174.

AVOID THE *Error*

When a polite request is phrased as a question, a question mark is needed.

✗ Can we receive the shipment by January 25.	✓ Can we receive the shipment by January 25?

We can also form polite requests with *I'd like.*

I'd like you to hang your coat in the closet. (In this situation, *I'd like* is stronger than *can* or *could.*)

I'd like is common in restaurants and other situations when you are ordering.

I'd like a large orange juice, please.

AVOID THE *Error*

In polite situations, use polite requests, not imperatives.

✗ **Give** us a table for two.	✓ **We'd like** a table for two.

Imperatives with *Have*

English uses *have* in many expressions in the imperative. We use these expressions to offer invitations and express hopes and wishes.

Have a seat.
Have a drink.
Have some more vegetables.
Have a safe trip!
Have a good day!
Have a good rest.
We hope you **have** happy holidays!

Exercise

A *Read each situation, and write an imperative or a polite request.*

1. You're hungry. There is a bowl of fruit near your friend. You want your friend to pass you an orange.

   ____

2. A child is hitting his sister. You want him to stop hitting his sister.

   ____

3. You're riding in a friend's car. The friend is speeding. You don't want him to speed.

   ____

4. You and a friend are going to go to the movies. You want to see *Transformers 3*.

   ____

5. It's very cold outside. A window is open. Your friend is near the window. You want her to close it.

   ____

6. You're at a restaurant. You want baked chicken. Make a polite request.

   ____

7. You want your children to put their shoes by the door. Make a polite request.

   ____

8. A guest is in your house. You want the person to have a seat.

   ____

9. You and a friend are shopping in a supermarket. You are both finished shopping and ready to check out.

   ____

10. A friend is leaving on a long car trip. You want to wish her a safe trip.

    ____

VERBS
Be: Simple Past Tense

We use the simple past tense of *be* to show a state or a quality of something in the past.

I **was** happy at the news.
They **were** late yesterday.

Formation

These tables show the affirmative and negative forms of the simple past tense of *be*:

AFFIRMATIVE

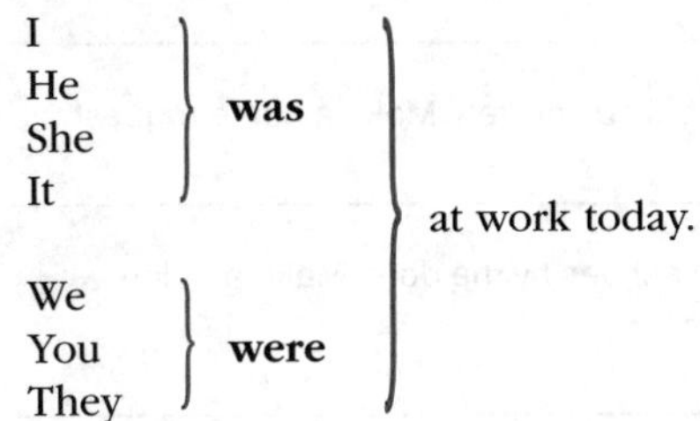

I
He
She
It
was

We
You
They
were

at work today.

NEGATIVE

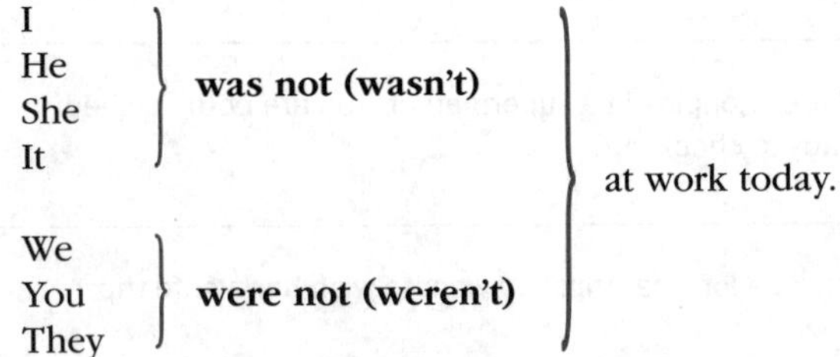

I
He
She
It
was not (wasn't)

We
You
They
were not (weren't)

at work today.

AVOID THE *Error*

Do not use *was* with *we*, *you*, and *they*; use *were*.

✗ They **was** late. ✓ They **were** late.

Questions with *Be* in the Simple Past Tense

Form questions with *be* in the simple past tense in the same way you form questions with *be* in the simple present tense.

You **were** at work today.	→	**Were** you at work today?
They **were** from China.	→	Where **were** they from?

For more information on the formation of questions with *be*, see page 126.

Exercise

A *Complete the sentences by writing the correct form of the verb on the line.*

1. Kelly ________________ a teacher at this school last year.
2. I ________________ (**not**) hungry at lunchtime, so I went to my car and took a nap.
3. Jason and Kate ________________ at the beach all day yesterday.
4. We ________________ very busy at work on Saturday.
5. My daughter ________________ sick yesterday and didn't go to school.
6. I saw a movie yesterday, but it ________________ (**not**) very good.
7. The weather ________________ cold yesterday.
8. We ________________ downtown this morning.
9. My train ________________ late yesterday.
10. Our hamburgers ________________ (**not**) very good.

VERBS
Simple Past Tense

We use the simple past tense to talk about actions that happened in the past and are completed or finished.

She **called** me this morning.
We **talked** for an hour.
We **finished** our call at 11:00.
Then I **walked** to work.

We also use the simple past tense to talk about habitual or repeated actions in the past.

When I was in high school, I **walked** to school every day.

We often use an adverb of time with a simple past-tense verb, such as *yesterday*, *last night*, *two weeks ago*, and so on.

I **washed** the car **last Sunday**.
She **bought** her new car **three weeks ago**.
Yesterday they **went** to the beach.

AVOID THE Error

Do not use the simple present tense in place of the simple past tense.

✘ They **go** to the beach yesterday.

✔ They **went** to the beach yesterday.

Formation

This table shows how to form the simple past tense of affirmative regular verbs:

Subject	Verb
I You He She It We They	**cooked** **walked** **cleaned**

This table shows how to form the simple past tense of affirmative irregular verbs:

Subject	Verb
I You He She It We They	**ran** **ate** **slept**

This table shows how to form the simple past tense of negative regular and irregular verbs:

Subject	Auxiliary	Verb
I You He She It We They	**did not (didn't)** **did not (didn't)**	**cook**. **eat**.

Use the past tense of the verb *do* (*did*) + *not* to form negatives. Add *did not* or *didn't*, and change the verb to the base form.

He **cooked** dinner.
He **didn't cook** dinner.

AVOID THE *Error*

Do not use the simple past-tense form of the main verb in negative sentences. Use the base form.

✗ Marty didn't **sent** the e-mail.	✓ Marty didn't **send** the e-mail.
✗ He didn't **went** to the store.	✓ He didn't **go** to the store.

Spelling Regular Simple-Past Verbs

Add *-d* to verbs that end in a vowel.

dance	➜	dance**d**
move	➜	move**d**
believe	➜	believe**d**
live	➜	live**d**

If a verb ends in a consonant + stressed vowel + consonant, double the consonant and add *-ed*.

stop	➜	sto**pp**ed
slip	➜	sli**pp**ed
plan	➜	pla**nn**ed

AVOID THE *Error*

Do *not* double a final consonant if the last syllable is *not* stressed.

✗ visit—visi**tt**ed	✔ visit—visi**t**ed
✗ listen—liste**nn**ed	✔ listen—liste**n**ed
✗ iron—iro**nn**ed	✔ iron—iro**n**ed

Don't double a final *w* or *x*. Just add *-ed*.

allow	➜	allow**ed**
snow	➜	snow**ed**
box	➜	box**ed**

If a verb ends in a consonant + *y*, drop the *y* and add *-ied*.

stud**y**	➜	stud**ied**
worr**y**	➜	worr**ied**
carr**y**	➜	carr**ied**
tr**y**	➜	tr**ied**

If a verb ends in a vowel + *y*, add *-ed*.

pla**y**	➜	play**ed**
sta**y**	➜	stay**ed**

Add *-ed* to all other verbs.

walk	→	walk**ed**
accept	→	accept**ed**
need	→	need**ed**
mail	→	mail**ed**
count	→	count**ed**
rain	→	rain**ed**

AVOID THE *Error*

Do not double a final consonant when there are two vowels before it.

✗ need—nee**dd**ed ✓ need—nee**d**ed

Do not drop a final *y* if a verb ends in vowel + *y*; just add *-ed*.

✗ stay—sta**i**ed ✓ stay—sta**y**ed

Pronouncing Regular Simple Past-Tense Verbs

The *-ed* ending is pronounced:

- /t/ after voiceless consonants such as /p, t, k, f, ʃ, tʃ/ (Your vocal chords do not vibrate when you say voiceless sounds.)

  stopped walked danced liked

- /d/ after vowels and voiced consonants such as /b, v, g, ʤ, z/ (Your vocal chords vibrate when you say vowels and voiced consonants.)

  played mailed allowed loved smiled

- /əd/ after /t/ and /d/

  accepted started tasted

For more information on voiced and voiceless consonants, see page 4.

Irregular Simple Past Verbs

Many verbs are irregular in the simple past tense, though some verbs fall into broad groups with similar changes. The following table summarizes the most common patterns:

BASE	SIMPLE PAST
beat	beat
cost	cost
cut	cut
hit	hit
hurt	hurt
let	let
put	put
lend	lent
spend	spent
build	built
lose	lost
bite	bit
hide	hid
eat	ate
fall	fell
forget	forgot
give	gave
see	saw
take	took
blow	blew
grow	grew
know	knew
throw	threw
fly	flew
draw	drew
begin	began
drink	drank
swim	swam
ring	rang
sing	sang
run	ran

keep	kept
sleep	slept
feel	felt
leave	left
meet	met
mean	meant
bring	brought
buy	bought
fight	fought
think	thought
catch	caught
teach	taught
sell	sold
tell	told
find	found
hear	heard
hold	held
say	said
stand	stood
understand	understood
drive	drove
ride	rode
write	wrote
break	broke
choose	chose
speak	spoke
steal	stole
wake	woke
ring	rang
sing	sang
run	ran
come	came
become	became

For an alphabetical list of irregular verbs, see the section "Irregular Verb List" at the end of the book.

AVOID THE *Error*

Do not use the regular simple-past tense ending with irregular verbs.

✗ His car **hitted** the other car at five miles per hour.	✓ His car **hit** the other car at five miles per hour.
✗ I **waked up** very early this morning.	✓ I **woke up** very early this morning.

Questions in the Simple Past Tense

Yes/No Questions

To form *yes/no* questions in the simple past, insert *did* before the subject, change the verb to the base form, and add a question mark:

I received a letter today. → **Did** you **receive** a letter today?

Wh- Questions

To form *wh-* questions in the simple past, insert a question word, insert *did* before the subject, change the verb to the base form, and add a question mark:

I bought this hat at the flea market. → **Where did** you **buy** this hat?

AVOID THE *Error*

Do not use the simple past-tense form of the main verb in questions. Use the base form.

✗ Did Mary **sent** the e-mail?	✓ Did Mary **send** the e-mail?
✗ When did he **went** to the store?	✓ When did he **go** to the store?

Used To

We can use the simple past tense with *used to* to describe past habits or actions that we no longer do.

He **used to** smoke, but he quit more than seven years ago.
I **used to** live on Mulberry Street.

AVOID THE *Error*

In questions, *used to* becomes *use to.*

✗	✓
Did you **used** to live on Mulberry Street?	**Did** you **use** to live on Mulberry Street?
Where did you **used** to live?	Where did you **use** to live?

Simple Past Tense for Politeness

Sometimes, English speakers will use the simple past tense instead of the present tense to show politeness or respect:

Did you **want** me to hand in my paper?
We **were wondering** if you are ready.

AVOID THE *Error*

Avoid shifts in tense. A shift in tense happens when a sentence or paragraph begins in one tense and then changes tense for no reason.

✗	✓
After we **arrived** at Disney World last year, we **checked** into our hotel. Later, we **will go** to the park and **see** the rides.	After we **arrived** at Disney World last year, we **checked** into our hotel. Later, we **went** to the park and **saw** the rides.

Exercises

A *Complete the sentences by writing the verb in parentheses in the simple past tense.*

1. Yesterday I ________________ (**write**) a long e-mail to my best friend.
2. The boss ________________ (**call**) an employee meeting on Sunday night.
3. I ________________ (**not drive**) to work today. I ________________ (**take**) the bus.
4. Frank ________________ (**use to**) live in Los Angeles.
5. Last year, my family ________________ (**go**) to Mexico on vacation.
6. I ________________ (**forget**) to buy milk at the supermarket.
7. The batter ________________ (**hit**) a home run, and the team ________________ (**win**) the baseball game.
8. It ________________ (**not rain**) yesterday, but it ________________ (**rain**) all day today.
9. Jack ________________ (**tell**) a lot of jokes, and we ________________ (**laugh**) at all of them.
10. I ________________ (**not cook**) dinner last night. We ________________ (**eat**) in a restaurant.
11. Last night I ________________ (**have**) a terrible dream.
12. Yesterday, Marta ________________ (**sleep**) late. She ________________ (**get**) up at 9:30.
13. Yesterday, I ________________ (**stay**) at work from 8:30 in the morning until 6:30 at night.
14. On Sunday, Mr. Fernandez ________________ (**start**) working on his income tax return. He finally ________________ (**finish**) on Tuesday night.
15. For breakfast, Tyrone ________________ (**have**) a cup of coffee and some cereal.
16. Last night I was very tired. I ________________ (**not watch**) TV. I ________________ (**go**) to bed very early.
17. Christine ________________ (**not understand**) the instructions, so she ________________ (**ask**) the teacher a question.

18. I ______________________ (**meet**) a lot of interesting people at the party last night.
19. After lunch, Vickie ______________________ (**wash**) the dishes.
20. We ______________________ (**try**) the new restaurant near our house. It's very good.

B *Read the conversations. Using the simple past tense, write B's questions.*

1. A: I had a great vacation.
   B: Where ______________________________ (**go**)?
   A: Florida.
2. A: I bought a new computer.
   B: How much ______________________________ (**cost**)?
   A: Only $500.
3. A: I made dinner last night.
   B: What ______________________________ (**cook**)?
   A: Spaghetti with meatballs.
4. A: Fred woke up early this morning.
   B: What time ______________________________ (**get up**)?
   A: 5:30.
5. A: I didn't go to work yesterday?
   B: Why ______________________________ (**not go**) to work?
   A: I was sick.

VERBS
Past Progressive Tense

We use the past progressive tense to talk about actions that were in progress in the past.

Last night I **was watching** old movies on TV.

We also use the past progressive tense to stress that an action took place for an extended period of time.

Last Thanksgiving, we **were cooking** all morning.

AVOID THE *Error*

Do not use the past progressive tense for habitual actions in the past. Use the simple past tense.

✘ Joanne **was watching** TV every night.

✔ Joanne **watched** TV every night last week.

Formation

The past progressive tense is formed with the past tense of *be* (*was* or *were*) and the present participle (verb + *-ing*). For information on spelling present participles, see page 138.

This table shows how to form affirmative and negative statements in the past progressive tense:

Subject	Verb	
I He She It	**was (not/wasn't)**	**going** to the store.
We You They	**were (not/weren't)**	

When and *While* and the Past Progressive Tense

We often use the past progressive tense with the simple past tense. The past progressive tense describes a longer action, while the simple past tense describes a shorter action. The shorter action interrupts or occurs during the longer action. We often use a clause with *while* to introduce the longer action. The clauses can come in any order.

While I was cooking dinner, the phone rang.
The phone rang **while** I was cooking dinner.

We can also use a clause with *when* to introduce the shorter action. The clauses can come in any order.

I was cooking dinner **when** the phone rang.
When the phone rang, I was cooking dinner.

AVOID THE Error

In sentences with a *when* or *while* clause, a comma is needed only if the clause with *when* or *while* is first in the sentence.

✗ While Anita was on the phone I sent a fax.	✓ While Anita was on the phone, I sent a fax.
✗ I sent a fax, while Anita was on the phone.	✓ I sent a fax while Anita was on the phone.

Questions in the Past Progressive Tense

Yes/No Questions

To form *yes/no* questions, invert *was* or *were* and the subject and add a question mark.

I was cooking all day on Thanksgiving. → **Were** you cooking all day on Thanksgiving?

Wh- Questions

To form *wh-* questions, add a question word, invert *was* or *were* and the subject and add a question mark.

I was cooking dinner when you called. → **What were** you doing when I called?

Exercises

A *Look at Joanne's schedule, and answer the questions.*

9:00 Get ready for work

9:30 Drive to work

10:00 Work

12:00 Eat lunch

5:00 Drive home

1. What was Joanne doing at 9:00?

 ____

2. What was she doing at 9:30?

 ____

3. What was she doing at 10:00?

 ____

4. What was she doing at 12:00?

 ____

5. What was she doing at 5:00?

 ____

B *Complete the sentences by writing the verb in parentheses in the simple past tense or past progressive tense.*

1. While I ____________ (**wash**) the dishes, I ____________ (**broke**) a glass.
2. She ____________ (**drive**) home when she ____________ (**have**) an accident.
3. When they ____________ (**hear**) the news, they ____________ (**listen**) to the radio.
4. We ____________ (**study**) English when Frank ____________ (**call**).
5. We ____________ (**ate**) popcorn while we ____________ (**watch**) the movie.

VERBS
Present Perfect Tense

We use the present perfect tense to talk about actions that began in the past and continue to the present.

I **have lived** in Chicago for seven years.

We also use the present perfect tense to talk about actions that have taken place from some indefinite time in the past up to the present.

I've been to Paris three times.

And we use the present perfect tense to describe actions that have been recently completed. We often use *just* to indicate that an action recently happened.

We**'ve just arrived.**

AVOID THE *Error*

Do not use the present perfect tense in place of the simple past tense. The present perfect is a present tense that describes actions that have continued to the present or are important now. The simple past tense describes actions that were completed and finished in the past.

✗ The Civil War **has ended** in 1865.

✓ The Civil War **ended** in 1865.

Formation

The present perfect tense is formed with the verb *have* (*have* or *has*) and the past participle.

AVOID THE *Error*

The verb *have* is irregular. Remember to use *has* when the subject is *he*, *she*, or *it*.

✘ He **have** lived here for many years.

✔ He **has** lived here for many years.

This table shows how the present perfect tense is formed:

Subject	Auxiliary	Participle
I We You They	**have ('ve) (not/haven't)**	**gone** to the store.
He She It	**has ('s) (not/hasn't)**	

AVOID THE *Error*

Use a complete verb phrase in the present perfect tense. Do not omit *have* or *has*.

✘ He **written** several e-mails today.

✔ He **has written** several e-mails today.

Use the contractions of *have* (*'s* and *'ve*) interchangeably with the full forms, *has* and *have*, in spoken English.

We'**ve** lived here for four years. We **have** lived here for four years.

AVOID THE *Error*

Do not use contractions of *have* in formal, written English.

✘ The President'**s** considered the matter, and he'**s** made a decision.

✔ The President **has** considered the matter, and he **has** made a decision.

Have is also a full verb. A full verb can stand alone. As a full verb, *have* means "possess or own." *Have* does not have contractions when used as a full verb.

AVOID THE *Error*

When *have* is a full verb, do not use contractions.

✘ They've a new car. ✔ They **have** a new car.

The contractions of *has* and *is* are the same: *'s*.

She's a teacher. (*'s* is a contraction of *is*)
She's been a teacher for twenty-seven years. (*'s* is a contraction of *has*)

AVOID THE *Error*

Avoid confusing contractions of *is* and *have* when you write the complete forms.

She'**s** visited Rome.	✘ She **is** visited Rome.	✔ She **has** visited Rome.
He'**s** reading a book.	✘ He **has** reading a book.	✔ He **is** reading a book.
Ed'**s** a nice guy.	✘ Ed **has** a nice guy.	✔ Ed **is** a nice guy.

Spelling Past Participles

With regular verbs, the simple past tense and the past participle are the same.

cook	→	cook**ed**
fix	→	fix**ed**
stop	→	stop**ped**
try	→	tr**ied**
play	→	play**ed**

With many irregular verbs, the simple past and past participle are also the same. This table summarizes irregular verbs whose simple past and past participles are the same:

BASE	SIMPLE PAST	PAST PARTICIPLE
cost	cost	cost
cut	cut	cut
hit	hit	hit
hurt	hurt	hurt
let	let	let
put	put	put
lend	lent	lent
spend	spent	spent
build	built	built
lose	lost	lost
keep	kept	kept
sleep	slept	slept
feel	felt	felt
leave	left	left
meet	met	met
mean	meant	meant
bring	brought	brought
buy	bought	bought
fight	fought	fought
think	thought	thought
catch	caught	caught
teach	taught	taught
sell	sold	sold
tell	told	told
find	found	found
hear	heard	heard
hold	held	held
say	said	said
stand	stood	stood
understand	understood	understood

With other irregular verbs, the simple past and the past participle are different. This table summarizes some of those verbs:

BASE	SIMPLE PAST	PAST PARTICIPLE
be	was, were	been
drive	drove	driven
ride	rode	ridden
write	wrote	written
break	broke	broken
choose	chose	chosen
speak	spoke	spoken
steal	stole	stolen
wake	woke	woken
blow	blew	blown
grow	grew	grown
know	knew	known
throw	threw	thrown
fly	flew	flown
draw	drew	drawn
begin	began	begun
drink	drank	drunk
swim	swam	swum
ring	rang	rung
sing	sang	sung
run	ran	run
come	came	come
become	became	become
bite	bit	bitten
hide	hid	hidden
eat	ate	eaten
fall	fell	fallen
forget	forgot	forgotten
give	gave	given
see	saw	seen
take	took	taken

The verb *read* is spelled the same in the present tense, simple past tense, and past participle forms, but is pronounced like the color word *red* in the past tense and past participle forms.

BASE	SIMPLE PAST	PAST PARTICIPLE
read	read ("red")	read ("red")

AVOID THE *Error*

Do not use a simple past-tense verb in the present perfect tense. Use the past participle.

✘ He's **began** to learn French. ✔ He's **begun** to learn French.

For a list of irregular verbs, see the Irregular Verb List at the back of the book.

Adverbs of Time with the Present Perfect Tense

We use certain adverbs of time with the present perfect tense.

For and *Since*

We use *for* and *since* to talk about how long an action has lasted from the past up until the present.

How long have you lived in Chicago?
I've lived in Chicago **for** seven years.
I've lived in Chicago **since** 2003.

AVOID THE *Error*

Do not use:

- **A period of time with *since*.** Give the starting time in the past.

✘ He's studied English since **two hours**. ✔ He's studied English since **eleven o'clock**.

- **A starting time in the past with *for*.** Give the period of time the action has taken place.

✘ He's studied English for **eleven o'clock**. ✔ He's studied English for **two hours**.

Already and *Yet*

We use *yet* to ask whether someone has completed an action up to now. We also use *yet* to say that we have not completed an action up to now. We use *already* to state that we have completed the action up to now.

Have you finished your ice cream **yet**?
No, we haven't finished our ice cream **yet**.
Yes, we've **already** finished our ice cream.

> **AVOID THE *Error***
>
> Do not use *yet* in affirmative sentences. Use *already*.
>
> ✘ The mechanic has fixed my car **yet**.
>
> ✔ The mechanic has **already** fixed my car.

Ever and *Never*

We use *ever* and *never* to talk about whether we have done an activity anytime up to the present.

Have you **ever** seen the President in person?
No, I've **never** seen the President in person.
Yes, I saw him give a speech last year.

> **AVOID THE *Error***
>
> In general, do not use *ever* in affirmative sentences. Only use it in questions.
>
> ✘ I have **ever** seen the President.
>
> ✔ I have seen the President.
>
> ✔ I have **never** seen the President.
>
> ✔ Have you **ever** seen the President?

We can use *ever* in sentences with superlative adjectives and the present perfect tense or simple past tense.

This is the biggest pumpkin I have **ever** seen.

AVOID THE *Error*

Do not use *never* in sentences with superlative adjectives and the present perfect tense or simple past tense. Use *ever.*

✘ He is the cheapest person I have **never** met.

✔ He is the cheapest person I have **ever** met.

Just

We use *just* to describe an action that was recently completed.

She's **just** arrived.

AVOID THE *Error*

Do not use an adverb of time such as *yesterday* or *last week*, which implies a completed action, with the present perfect tense. If the action is not yet completed or is recently completed, remove the adverb. If the action is completed, keep the adverb and use the simple past tense.

✘ We have arrived at ten o'clock.

✔ We have arrived. (action recently completed)

✔ We arrived at ten o'clock. (action completed in the past)

Questions in the Present Perfect Tense

Yes/No Questions

To form *yes/no* questions, invert *have* or *has* and the subject, and add a question mark.

They have washed the dishes. → **Have** they washed the dishes?

Wh- Questions

To form *wh-* questions, add a question word, invert *have* or *has* and the subject, and add a question mark.

He has lived in that apartment for two years.	→ **How long has** he lived in that apartment?

AVOID THE *Error*

The contraction for *who has* is *who's*, not *whose.*

✘ **Whose** left already?	✔ **Who's** left already?

Who's is also the contraction for *who is.* Do not confuse these when you write the full forms.

Who's your favorite actor?	✘ Who **has** your favorite actor? ✔ Who **is** your favorite actor?
Who's been to Rome?	✘ Who **is** been to Rome? ✔ Who **has** been to Rome?

Exercises

A *Complete the sentences by writing the correct form of the verb in the present perfect tense.*

1. I __________________ (**live**) in Chicago for five years.
2. I think that the boss __________________ (**leave**) work for the day. He'll be back tomorrow at 9 o'clock.
3. __________________ you __________________ (**try**) this ice cream? It's delicious!
4. We __________________ (**know**) Mr. Robinson for more than thirty years. He's our nicest neighbor.
5. Ellen __________________ (**work**) for this company for more than nine years.
6. I __________________ (**wait**) for this bus for forty-five minutes. I'm going to take a taxi, or I'll be late for work.
7. We __________________ (**be**) married for five years.
8. He __________________ just __________________ (**finish**) painting the baby's bedroom.

9. ________ you ________ (**see**) his new apartment? It's beautiful.
10. They ________ (**not arrive**) yet. They'll get here in a few minutes.
11. Oh, no! I think I ________ (**lose**) my driver's license.
12. The bell ________ (**ring**). It's time to start class.
13. I ________ already ________ (**read**) all the Harry Potter books.
14. She ________ (**buy**) some new jeans, but she ________ (**not wear**) them yet.
15. He ________ (**have**) many jobs during his career.
16. I ________ (**write**) three letters to friends in my country today.
17. We ________ never ________ (**fly**) in a plane in our lives!
18. How long ________ you ________ (**live**) in Chicago?
19. He ________ (**not drink**) coffee for more than ten years.
20. We ________ (**find**) a lost dog in the park.

B *Write* ever, never, already, yet, for, *or* since *on the line. If no word is required, write* X.

1. A: Have you ________ visited Paris?

   B: No, I've ________ visited Paris, but I've been to Mexico City several times.
2. A: Have you finished your homework ________?

   B: No, I haven't finished my homework ________. I still have a few things to do.
3. A: Have you started cooking dinner ________?

   B: Yes, I've ________ started cooking dinner.
4. A: How long have you worked here?

   B: I've worked here ________ 2001.

   A: Wow! You've worked here ________ a long time.
5. A. Have you ________ lived in California?

   B: Yes, I've ________ lived in California.

VERBS
Future Tense with *Going to* and *Will*

We can talk about the future in several ways. We can use:

- **The simple present tense** to talk about future actions that are a part of a schedule

  My plane **leaves** tomorrow morning at 9:30.

- **The present progressive tense** to talk about future plans

  On my way home, **I'm stopping** at the supermarket and the gas station.

We also use:

- ***Going to*** or ***will*** to talk about predictions about the future

  Tomorrow it **is going to rain**. Tomorrow it **will rain**.

- ***Going to*** to talk about plans for the future

  I'm tired of cooking. Tonight I **am going to eat** dinner out.

- ***Will*** (or its contraction ***'ll***) to make promises about the future

  After lunch, **I'll buy** you some ice cream. After lunch, I **will buy** you some ice cream.

AVOID THE *Error*

People often pronounce *going to* as "gonna." Use *gonna* in informal speech. In writing and more formal speech, use *going to.*

✗ I'm **gonna** do the laundry tomorrow.

✓ I'm **going to** do the laundry tomorrow.

Formation

This table shows how to form sentences with *will*:

Subject	Verb	
I / He / She / It / We / You / They	**will ('ll)** / **will not (won't)**	**cook** dinner tonight.

AVOID THE Error

Use the apostrophe correctly in the contraction *won't*. The apostrophe replaces the missing *o* in *not*.

✘ I **w'ont** be at work on time tomorrow. I have to go to the dentist first.

✔ I **won't** be at work on time tomorrow. I have to go to the dentist first.

This table shows how to form sentences with *going to*:

Subject	Verb	Negative	
I	**am ('m)**	**(not)**	**going to cook** dinner tonight.
He / She / It	**is ('s)**	**(not/isn't)**	
We / You / They	**are ('re)**	**(not/aren't)**	

AVOID THE Error

Do not omit a form of the verb *be* (*am*, *is*, or *are*) in sentences with *going to*.

✘ She going to make spaghetti for dinner.

✔ She **is** going to make spaghetti for dinner.

Questions with *Going to* and *Will*

Yes/No Questions

To form *yes/no* questions, invert *be* (*is* or *are*) or *will* and the subject, and add a question mark.

They're going to buy a new car. ➜ **Are they** going to buy a new car?

I will marry you. ➜ **Will you** marry me?

Wh- Questions

To form *wh-* questions, add a question word, invert *be* or *will* and the subject, and add a question mark.

He is going to arrive in a few minutes. ➜ **When is** he going to arrive?

I'll park my car near the main entrance. ➜ **Where will you** park your car?

Exercises

A *Complete the sentences by using* going to *with the verb in parentheses.*

1. Tomorrow, it ______________________ (**rain**).
2. I ______________________ (**get up**) early and go swimming every day this week.
3. We ______________________ (**go**) shopping Saturday morning.
4. I ______________________ (**do**) the laundry this afternoon.
5. They ______________________ (**eat**) dinner in a few minutes.

B *Complete the sentences by using* will *with the verb in parentheses.*

1. I am sure the test ______________________ (**be**) difficult.
2. The party ______________________ (**take**) place on Saturday night.
3. Explain the problem to him. I am sure that he ______________________ (**understand**).
4. I ______________________ (**send**) you a postcard from Mexico.
5. I hope you ______________________ (**have**) lunch with us tomorrow.

VERBS
Modal Verbs

A modal verb is used with another verb to express ability, permission, obligation and prohibition, necessity, requests, offers and invitations, speculation, and advice.

I **can** speak three languages. (ability)
You **may** go to the library. (permission)
You **must** pay your taxes by April 15. (obligation)
He **might** be lost. (speculation)
You **should** arrive on time every day. (advice)

AVOID THE *Error*

Do not add *-s*, *-ed*, or *-ing* to modal verbs.

✘ He **cans** drive a motorcycle.	✔ He **can** drive a motorcycle.
✘ He **canned** speak three languages.	✔ He **could** speak three languages.
✘ He **musted** get his car fixed.	✔ He **had to** get his car fixed.

Formation

Modal verbs include:

can	could	may	might
must	should	ought to	would

AVOID THE Error

The modal verbs *can, could, may, might, must, should,* or *would* are followed by the base form of a verb. Do not use *to* after these modal verbs. Use the base form of the verb without *to.* Do not add *-s, -ed,* or *-ing* to the base form of the verb.

✘ They can **to** come to the party. ✔ They can come to the party.

✘ She might **bringing** a friend to the party. ✔ She might **bring** a friend to the party.

Use *to* after *ought.*

✘ You ought wash your car. ✔ You ought **to** wash your car.

Do not add *-s, -ed,* or *-ing* to the infinitive that follows *ought.*

✘ She ought to **cutting** the lawn. ✔ She ought to **cut** the lawn.

To form the negative forms of modal verbs, insert *not* or *-n't* after the modal verb.

I ca**n't** dance very well.
You should**n't** go to bed so late on a work night.

AVOID THE Error

Can + *not* is written as one word: *cannot.*

✘ You **can not** park in front of a fire hydrant. ✔ You **cannot** park in front of a fire hydrant.

Meanings of Modal Verbs

A modal verb can have more than one meaning. Here are the meanings of the main modal verbs.

Can and *Could*

Can expresses an ability in the present. *Could* expresses ability in the past.

I **can** dance, but I **can't** sing.
When I was twenty, I **could** dance all night.
I **couldn't** finish my dinner, because I had a stomachache.

AVOID THE *Error*

To express ability in the future, use *able to*, not *can*.

✗ After using this book, you **can** speak English accurately.

✓ After using this book, you **will be able to** speak English accurately.

Can and *could* express requests in the present and the future.

Can you help me with my math homework?
Could you bring me a cup of coffee?

Can expresses permission in the present or future.

You **can** use this computer to send e-mail.
John, you **can't** stay out past 10:30 tonight.

AVOID THE *Error*

Normally, we don't turn down a request with "No, you can't," or "No, you couldn't," without giving a reason or more information.

Can I go to the movies with Mark?

✗ No, you can't.

✓ No you can't. You have to do your homework.

Can and *could* express possibility in the present or future.

If we have time, we **can** go to the mall after the movie.
We **could** get some ice cream after dinner.

Could expresses a suggestion in the present or future.

We **could** have a mechanic check that used car before we buy it.

AVOID THE *Error*

Modal verbs cannot be used as infinitives. Use a verb or an expression with a related meaning. For example, for *can*, use *to be able to.*

✗ I hope to **can** go to the movies tonight.

✓ I hope **to be able to** go to the movies tonight.

Must

Must expresses an obligation in the present or future.

You **must** wear a seat belt when you are in a car.
You **must not** smoke in a movie theater.

The opposite of *must* is *don't have to.*

You **don't have to** take the bus to work. You can walk, drive, or take the subway.

To talk about an obligation in the past, use *had to*:

I **had to** file my tax return yesterday.

Have to has a meaning similar to *must*, but *have to* is not a modal. It has a past-tense form (*had to*) and is followed by an infinitive, not a base verb.

We **have to** leave now.
Our car wouldn't start, so we **had to** call a tow truck.

Should and *Ought To*

The modal verbs *should* and *ought to* make recommendations or suggestions.

You **should** get eight hours of sleep every night.
You **shouldn't** stay out late at night before work.
You **ought to** visit your mother more often.

AVOID THE *Error*

The negative form of *ought to* is *oughtn't to*, but English speakers normally do not use this form. Use *should not* or *shouldn't* instead.

✗ You **oughtn't to** drive so fast. ✓ You **shouldn't** drive so fast.

Had better is also used to make recommendations or suggestions. Generally, *had better* is a stronger recommendation than *ought to* or *should*. The contraction for *had better* is *'d better*.

You'**d better** hurry up, or you'll be late for work!
You'**d better not** be late for work again, or you'll get fired!

Would

We use *would* to talk about what was going to happen in the past.

He said that he **would** come.

The contraction of *would* is *'d*.

He said he'**d** come.

AVOID THE *Error*

The contraction *'d* can stand for *had* or *would*. Be careful when writing the full form.

He said he'**d** help us.	✗ He said he **had** help us. ✓ He said he **would** help us.
He said he'**d** arrived	✗ He said he **would** arrived. ✓ He said he **had** arrived.

We use *would like* (or its contraction *'d like)* to make polite offers and requests.

I'd like a double cheeseburger, please.
Would you **like** fries with that?

AVOID THE *Error*

Do not confuse *'d like* (*want*) with *like* (*prefer*).

✗ I'd **like** milk. ✓ I **like** milk. (a preference)

✗ I **like** milk. ✓ **I'd like** milk. (a request)

Would expresses repeated actions in the past.

Every winter we **would** go sledding and skating.

May and *Might*

May expresses permission in the present or future.

You **may** have another piece of cake.
You **may** not go out after ten o'clock at night.

AVOID THE *Error*

May is not normally used in ordinary speech to talk about permission. Most speakers use *can.*

✗ May I go skateboarding after dinner? ✓ Can I go skateboarding after dinner?

Might expresses an optional action in the future or present.

If you miss the bus, you **might** take a cab to work.
You **might** add a bit of lemon juice to your iced tea.

May and *might* express possibility in the present and future. Generally, *may* is considered more likely than *might.*

Where is Mike? He **may** be in the bedroom.
Tomorrow it **might** rain.

AVOID THE *Error*

Do not confuse *may be* (modal verb *may* and verb *be*) with *maybe* (an adverb expressing uncertainty).

✗ He **maybe** outside.	✔ He **may be** outside.
✗ **May be** he's sick.	✔ **Maybe** he's sick.

Must Be, Could Be, Might Be

Three modal verb + *be* combinations express speculation.

John is absent today. He **must be** sick. (very certain)
John is absent today. He **could be** sick. (somewhat certain)
John is absent today. He **might be** sick. (not very certain)

To speculate that something is not the case, use *can't be* or *couldn't be.*

Mr. Fox has been in the hospital for days. He **can't be** well.
George left for the store ten minutes ago. He **couldn't be** back already.

Polite Requests with *May, Can,* and *Could*

We can make polite requests with *may*, *can*, and *could.*

May I have a glass of water?
Can I have some sugar for my coffee?
Could you pass me the salt, please?

Normally, we agree to these requests with words such as:

Of course.
Sure.
Yes, you can (may).

AVOID THE *Error*

Normally, people do not turn down polite requests with "No, you can't," "No, you may not," or "No, you couldn't," which listeners interpret as impolite. Instead, give a reason.

Can/Could/May I have some stamps?

✗ No, you **can't**.
✗ No, you **may** not.
✗ No, you **could not**.

✓ Sorry, but we're out of stamps right now.

✓ Sorry, but we don't have stamps right now.

For more information on polite requests, see page 142.

When *can/could*, *will/would*, or *may/might* follow another clause + *that*, such as "he says that," use *can*, *will*, or *may* if the first verb is in the present tense. Use *could*, *would*, or *might* if the first verb is in the past tense.

Malcolm **says** that he **will** come.
Malcolm **said** that he **would** come.

If Malcolm said that he is coming, and the speaker and listener are still waiting for Malcolm to arrive, they might say:

Malcolm said that he **will** come.

Questions with Modal Verbs

To form *yes/no* questions with modal verbs, invert the subject and the modal verb, and add a question mark. For *wh-* questions, insert a question word, invert the subject and modal verb, and add a question mark.

Can you help me shovel the snow?
Where can I buy some stamps?

For questions where the question word is the subject, do not invert the subject and modal verb.

Who can help me fix dinner?

AVOID THE *Error*

Do not use *do* or forms of *do* to form questions or negatives with modal verbs.

✗ Maria **doesn't can** drive. ✓ Maria **can't** drive.

✗ **Do you can** drive? ✓ **Can you** drive?

Exercises

A *Complete the sentences by using* can, can't, could, *or* couldn't.

1. John ______________________________ drive. He doesn't have a driver's license.
2. Frank lived in Beijing for ten years, so he ______________________________ speak Chinese very well.
3. My youngest son is only eleven months old, and he ______________________________ already walk.
4. Before I moved to Spain, I ______________________________ speak Spanish at all, but now I ______________________________ speak it very well.
5. John was sick today, so he ______________________________ go to work.
6. I am sorry, but you ______________________________ smoke in this restaurant. Please put out your cigarette.
7. I had to work, so I ______________________________ go to Mavis's party last night.
8. Good news! The mechanic says that he ______________________________ fix your car in an hour.
9. I have a terrible toothache. I hope I ______________________________ see the dentist today.
10. Yesterday, we ______________________________ go for a hike. The weather was terrible.

B *Complete the sentences by using* must, must not, had to, *or* don't have to.

1. You ______________________________ turn on the printer before you use it.
2. Today is a holiday, so I ______________________________ go to work.

3. Yesterday I ______________________ go to the dentist.
4. Ben and Luke hiked for miles today. They ______________________ be very tired.
5. Employees ______________________ use the guest parking lot. They can use employee parking lots A and B.

C *Complete the sentences by using* should, shouldn't, *or* would.

1. We ______________________ finish cleaning the kitchen before we watch TV.
2. ______________________ you like cream or sugar with your coffee?
3. Tim said that he ______________________ arrive at 8:30.
4. You ______________________ lock your bike, or someone will steal it.
5. When I lived in New York, I ______________________ take the subway to work every day.
6. He ______________________ drink so much coffee! I think he drinks more than ten cups a day.

D *Complete the sentences by circling the correct modal verb.*

1. I think we (**can/would**) go to the beach tomorrow.
2. When we were young, we (**would/must**) play baseball after school every day.
3. I (**like/would** like) a slice of apple pie, please.
4. You (**must/must not**) wear a seat belt in a car.
5. To stay healthy, you (**should/would**) eat a diet low in sugar and fat.
6. (**Could/Should**) you pass me the salt, please?
7. Mary Jane's doctor says that she (**must/must not**) stop smoking right away.
8. John stayed up all night studying for the test. He (**must/would**) be sleepy.
9. This computer isn't working? You (**might/would**) try the computer in the hall.
10. It (**might/must**) rain tomorrow.
11. It looks like rain. You (**should/would**) take an umbrella with you.
12. Peggy (**couldn't/must not**) go on vacation in Spain this year.
13. Young children (**should/shouldn't**) stay up past 11:00 at night.
14. (**Can/Would**) I use your mobile phone for a moment?

15. It's raining, so we (**can't/can**) go on a picnic.
16. I (**can't/couldn't**) go out with my friends last night. I had to work.
17. You (**could/should**) arrive at the airport at least an hour before your plane departs.
18. We (**may/would**) go to England next year on vacation.
19. John (**might not/could not**) work late yesterday. He had a doctor's appointment after work.
20. You (**ought/should**) to get more sleep.

VERBS
Subject-Verb Agreement

Subjects and verbs should match, or *agree*: singular subjects need singular verbs and plural subjects need plural verbs.

Abbie loves her dogs. (singular subject and verb)
John and Larry are farmers. (plural subject and verb)

AVOID THE *Error*

Singular nouns that end in *-s*, such as *politics*, *news*, *gymnastics*, and *mathematics*, need a singular verb.

✗ I think that mathematics **are** fascinating.
✔ I think that mathematics **is** fascinating.

✗ The news **are** on TV at 6:00.
✔ The news **is** on TV at 6:00.

AVOID THE *Error*

Verbs should agree with the subject of the sentence and not with nouns in phrases or clauses that come between the subject and the verb.

✗ The causes of the accident **was** analyzed by the police.
✔ The causes of the accident **were** analyzed by the police.

✗ The drivers who caused the accident **is** in jail.
✔ The drivers who caused the accident **are** in jail.

Sometimes subject-verb agreement can be tricky, such as in the following situations:

■ In impersonal expressions with *there*, *there* is not the subject. The noun that follows the verb is the subject, and the verb agrees with that noun.

There **is** a snake under the table.
There **are** some snakes under the table.

AVOID THE *Error*

In impersonal expressions with *there*, the verb agrees with the subject of the sentence. The subject of the sentence may not be the word closest to the verb.

✗	✓
There **is** several reasons for my decision.	There **are** several reasons for my decision. (*Reasons* is the subject.)
There **are** often more than one cause of these kinds of problems.	There **is** often more than one cause of these kinds of problems. (*Cause* is the subject.)

For more information on impersonal expressions with *there*, see pages 268–269.

■ A compound subject consists of two nouns joined by *and*. A compound subject is plural and has a plural verb.

Madonna and Prince are my favorite singers.

AVOID THE *Error*

Not all subjects joined with *and* are plural.

✗	✓
Early rock and roll **are** my favorite music.	Early rock and roll **is** my favorite music.

■ Collective nouns are nouns that include groups of people, animals, and objects but are considered singular and take singular verbs. Collective nouns include *team*, *committee*, *family*, *class*, *pack*, and *herd*.

Our team **is** winning!
My family always **orders** vegetarian pizza on Friday nights.
A herd of elephants **lives** in this zoo.

AVOID THE *Error*

Police is always plural, so it needs a plural verb.

✗ The police **is** investigating the robbery.	✔ The police **are** investigating the robbery.

- The words *somebody, anyone, nobody, someone, no one, either, neither, everyone, everybody, anybody, each,* and *each one* are singular and need singular verbs.

Nobody knows the future.
Someone ate all the doughnuts.
Everyone is here.

AVOID THE *Error*

Do not use plural verbs with words such as *somebody, anyone, nobody, someone, no one, either, neither, everyone, everybody, anybody, each,* and *each one.*

✗ Either John or Mary **are** in the kitchen.	✔ Either John or Mary **is** in the kitchen.

AVOID THE *Error*

No one is written as two words, not one.

✗ **Noone** knows where Mary Jane is.	✔ **No one** knows where Mary Jane is.

- The indefinite pronouns *both, few, many, others,* and *several* are plural.

Both are important.
Few people are here.

■ A few indefinite pronouns are singular or plural, depending on the use: *all*, *any*, *more*, *most*, and *some*.

All the neighbors are invited to the block party. (*Neighbors* is plural.)
All the furniture is covered in dust. (*Furniture* is an uncountable noun.)

■ Many grammar books say that *none* is singular because it means "not one."

None of the girls **is** here.

However, in ordinary speech, people often use a plural verb with *none*.

None of the girls **are** here.

■ *Money* is an uncountable noun, so it takes a singular verb.

Money **isn't** everything, but **it** sure makes life easier.

AVOID THE *Error*

The word *dollars* is plural, but it takes a singular verb when it is used to indicate an amount of money.

✗ I can't believe that twelve dollars **are** the cost of a movie ticket!	✓ I can't believe that twelve dollars **is** the cost of a movie ticket!

However, people sometimes use *dollars* with a plural verb when talking about amounts of money.

✓ Here **are** twelve dollars.

✓ Here **is** twelve dollars.

■ Words such as *scissors*, *pants*, *trousers*, and *pajamas* are plural, so they take plural verbs.

The scissors **are** on the table.

AVOID THE *Error*

When we use *pair of* with *scissors*, *pants*, *trousers*, and *pajamas*, the word *pair* is the subject and takes a singular verb.

✘ That new **pair** of pants **look** great!	✔ That new **pair** of pants **looks** great!

- Numbers are usually plural.

Five **are** here.

However, in some cases, a singular verb is used if we imagine the number as a unit of something.

Eight **is** enough.
Ten **is** plenty.
Two miles **is** not long for a hike.

AVOID THE *Error*

Total, *number*, and *majority* can be singular or plural depending on the words that follow them.

✘ A number of students **was** absent.	✔ A number of students **were** absent.
✘ The number of students absent **were** surprising.	✔ The number of students absent **was** surprising.
✘ The majority **rule**.	✔ The majority **rules**.
✘ A majority of the voters **opposes** the proposal.	✔ A majority of the voters **oppose** the proposal.
✘ A total of five students **wants** to see the movie.	✔ A total of 5 students **want** to see the movie.
✘ The total you owe **are** small.	✔ The total you owe **is** small.

Exercise

A *Circle the correct form of the verb.*

1. I think that politics (**is/are**) fascinating.
2. That pair of pajamas (**is/are**) very old. Let's throw them away.
3. A pack of wild, bloodthirsty wolves (**live/lives**) on Bald Mountain.
4. The girls in the red car (**is/are**) going with us to the party.
5. There (**is/are**) some good news for you in your e-mail today.

VERBS
Passive Voice

We use the active voice to give importance to the subject of the sentence.

John sold that car weeks ago.
The barking scared off the robbers.

We use the passive voice to give importance to the action.

That car **was sold** weeks ago.
The robbers **were scared off**.

Only transitive verbs can be used in passive-voice sentences. Transitive verbs can have direct or indirect objects. This table shows active- and passive-voice sentences with direct and indirect objects:

ACTIVE	PASSIVE
Thieves **stole** the painting.	The painting **was stolen**.
He **told** her the news yesterday.	She **was told** the news yesterday.
	The news **was told** to her yesterday.

For more information on transitive verbs, see page 120.

AVOID THE *Error*

Intrintransitive verbs, which do not have objects, cannot be used in the passive voice.

✗ The meeting **was taken** place. (passive voice)

✔ The meeting **took** place yesterday. (active voice)

Formation

To form the passive voice:

- The subject is deleted.
- The object of the verb becomes the subject of the passive sentence.
- A form of the verb *be* is added.
- The main verb becomes a past participle.

Here are some examples of active-voice and passive-voice (in bold) sentences.

John sold that car weeks ago. ➜ That car **was sold** weeks ago.
The barking scared off the robbers. ➜ The robbers **were scared** off.

For a list of past participles, see pages 164–165.

If a verb has a direct object and an indirect object, either one can become the subject (bold) of the passive-voice sentence:

We gave the retirees gold watches. ➜ **Gold** watches were given to the retirees.
➜ **The retirees** were given gold watches.

AVOID THE Error

When an object pronoun of an active-voice sentence becomes the subject of a passive-voice sentence, change the object pronoun to a subject pronoun.

I helped **her**. ➜ ✗ **Her** was helped. ✓ **She** was helped.

To form the passive voice:

- **In the simple present or simple past.** Use a form of *be* and the past participle of the main verb.

This restaurant **serves** homemade soup daily. ➜ Homemade soup **is served** daily.
They **served** eight different kinds of soup yesterday. ➜ Eight different kinds of soup **were served** yesterday.

- **In the present progressive tense or the past progressive tense.** Use a form of *be*, the present participle *being*, and the past participle of the main verb.

  Workers **are cleaning** the plane. → The plane **is being cleaned**.

- **In the present perfect tense.** Use *have* or *has*, the past participle of *be* (*been*), and the past participle of the main verb.

  The company **has fired** her. → She **has been fired**.

- **With modal verbs (including the future tense with *will*).** Use the modal verb, the verb *be*, and the past participle of the main verb.

  We **can't find** the keys. → The keys **can't be found**.

- **With *going to*.** Use a form of *be*, *going to be*, and the past participle of the main verb.

  We **are going to cook** the food now. → The food **is going to be cooked** now.

- **With an infinitive.** Add *be* before the infinitive.

  He's going **to help** her. → She's going **to be** helped.

This table summarizes the forms of active- and passive-voice verbs:

VERB FORM	ACTIVE VOICE	PASSIVE VOICE
Simple Present	Mark **cleans** the kitchen.	The kitchen **is cleaned**.
Present Progressive	Mark **is cleaning** the kitchen.	The kitchen **is being cleaned**.
Present Perfect	Mark **has cleaned** the kitchen.	The kitchen **has been cleaned**.
Simple Past	Mark **cleaned** the kitchen.	The kitchen **was cleaned**.
Past Progressive	Mark **was cleaning** the kitchen.	The kitchen **was being cleaned**.
Simple Future	Mark **will clean** the kitchen.	The kitchen **will be cleaned**.
Going to	Mark **is going to clean** the kitchen.	The kitchen **is going to be cleaned**.
Modal Verbs	Mark **can clean** the kitchen.	The kitchen **can be cleaned**.
	Mark **would clean** the kitchen.	The kitchen **would be cleaned**.

AVOID THE *Error*

Do not omit *be* from passive-voice sentences.

✘ Lincoln assassinated in 1865. ✔ Lincoln **was** assassinated in 1865.

To state the doer of the action in a passive-voice sentence, use the subject of the active-voice sentence in a phrase with *by*.

John delivered those pizzas. → Those pizzas were delivered **by John**.

Sabrina typed this document. → This document was typed **by Sabrina**.

AVOID THE *Error*

When the subject of an active-voice sentence is a pronoun and it moves to a *by*-phrase in a passive-voice sentence, change the subject pronoun to an object pronoun.

I called her. → ✘ She was called by **I**. ✔ She was called by **me**.

Indirect objects from an active-voice sentence can be stated in a passive-voice sentence with *to* or *for*.

The girls bought a present **for** Alice.
The girls gave a present **to** Alice.

AVOID THE *Error*

Sometimes the noun that follows *to* or *for* is not an indirect object. Rather, the prepositional phrase is really an adverb. When the prepositional phrase is an adverb, the noun cannot become the subject of a passive-voice sentence. Only the direct and indirect objects can become the subjects of a passive-voice sentence.

Active: After the accident, the insurance company gave me money **for a new car**.

Passive:

✗ A new car was given money for to me.

✓ **I** was given money for a new car. (indirect object)

✓ **Money** was given to me for a new car. (direct object)

Expressing the doer of the action in a *by* phrase is optional.

For selling the most cars this month, Mr. Baldus was given a free trip to Jamaica **by the sales manager**.
For selling the most cars this month, Mr. Baldus was given a free trip to Jamaica.

AVOID THE *Error*

Because the passive voice focuses on the action, and not on the doer of the action, we usually do not state the doer of the action in a *by* phrase. Avoid stating the doer of the action in passive-voice sentences. If stating the subject is important, consider using the active voice instead.

✗ The packages were all mailed this morning **by Gerardo**.

✓ The packages were all mailed this morning.

✓ **Gerardo** mailed all the packages this morning.

Sometimes, the meaning of the sentence changes slightly in the passive voice.

Many people attended the party.
The party was **well-attended**.

AVOID THE Error

When the doer of the action uses a tool to complete the action, use a phrase with *with* to show the tool.

✗ The vegetables were sliced **by a sharp knife.**

✔ The vegetables were sliced **with a sharp knife**. (The chef used the knife to cut the vegetables.)

✗ The drainpipe was opened **by a heavy-duty pipe wrench.**

✔ The drainpipe was opened **with a heavy-duty pipe wrench**. (A plumber used the pipe wrench.)

When a tool or object does the action itself, use a phrase with *by*.

✗ She was cut **with flying glass.**

✔ She was cut **by flying glass.** (Flying glass cut her.)

Uses of the Passive Voice

We use the passive voice when:

- We are more concerned about the action or the receiver of the action than about the doer.

  In Maine Park, more than two hundred trees **were damaged** by the storm.
  An oak tree more than four hundred years old **was** completely **destroyed** by the storm.

AVOID THE Error

Reflexive verbs are not used in the passive voice.

✗ She **was** accidentally **cut** by herself.

✔ She accidentally **cut herself.**

- The subject is unknown or indefinite.

  Rome **wasn't built** in a day.
  The explosion **was heard** all over the city.

- We want to avoid assigning responsibility for something.

  His car **was totaled** in the accident.
  Your application **will be reviewed,** and you **will be informed** of the outcome.

- The subject is vague or unknown.

  English **is understood** in most hotels around the world.
  This form **needs to be signed**.

AVOID THE *Error*

Do not overuse the passive voice. The passive voice is acceptable in speech and informal writing. But good writers avoid the passive voice in more formal kinds of writing, such as business letters and school papers, when it's possible to use the active voice. Overuse of the passive voice makes writing flat and uninteresting. Use the active voice instead.

✘ That new house was put up in about three months. First a big hole was dug. Then cement was poured to make the foundation. After that, brick walls were built. Finally, the roof was put on. The house was moved into about a month ago.

✔ The builders put up that new house in about three months. First, workers dug a big hole. Then a cement truck poured cement to make the foundation. After that, bricklayers built the walls. Finally, carpenters and roofers put the roof on. A family moved into the house about a month ago.

The *Get* Passive

We can use a form of the verb *get* and a past participle to form passive-voice sentences. We use the "*get* passive" in informal English.

Fred **got robbed.**
They **got hurt** in the accident.
We **got invited** to the party.
The students **are getting confused**.
Max **got fired**.

AVOID THE *Error*

Avoid using the *get* passive in formal, written English.

✘ The shipment will **get processed** in the warehouse and delivered to the customer by noon tomorrow.

✔ The shipment will **be processed** in the warehouse and delivered to the customer by noon tomorrow.

Exercises

A *Complete the passive-voice sentences by writing the correct form of the verb* be.

1. Marta calls Jean. Jean ______________ called.
2. Marta is calling Jean. Jean ______________ called.
3. Marta has called Jean. Jean ______________ called.
4. Marta called Jean. Jean ______________ called.
5. Marta was calling Jean. Jean ______________ called.
6. Marta will call Jean. Jean ______________ called.
7. Marta is going to call Jean. Jean ______________ called.
8. Marta can call Jean. Jean ______________ called.
9. Marta could call Jean. Jean ______________ called.
10. Marta might call Jean. Jean ______________ called.

B *Rewrite the sentences in the passive voice. Do not use a* by *phrase.*

1. She wrote that song in 1986.

____

2. Someone made a great suggestion at the meeting.

____

3. Workers made this jacket in France.

____

4. I hurt her feelings.

____

5. We will serve dinner at six o'clock sharp.

____

6. Someone has stolen my computer.

____

7. You should return this DVD to the library in two weeks.

____

8. We didn't close the windows last night.

____

9. People often misunderstand him.

____

10. We finished all the work.

____

C *Write the verb in the passive voice, using the correct verb tense.*

1. The U.S. Declaration of Independence ______________ (**sign**) in 1776.
2. Next year, a new shopping mall ______________ (**build**) in the middle of town.
3. Delicious soft ice cream ______________ (**serve**) in this restaurant every summer.
4. Three people ______________ (**hurt**) in yesterday's accident.
5. The whole city ______________ (**can see**) from the top of that skyscraper.
6. The door ______________ (**lock**) since 3:30 this afternoon.
7. Right now dinner ______________ (**cook**). We will eat in about an hour.
8. How much pizza ______________ (**should order**) to serve all the guests?
9. Last week I ______________ (**offer**) a new job, but I didn't take it.
10. Over the years, McDonald's ______________ (**sell**) billions of hamburgers.

VERBS
Two-Word Verbs

English has many two-word verbs. Sometimes these are called "phrasal verbs." They are formed with a verb plus a preposition or adverb.

He **woke up** at 5:30 yesterday.
Then he **turned over** and went back to sleep.
Please **sit down**.
He **got out** of the car.

Like other verbs, two-word verbs can have an object.

Let's turn on **the headlights**.
Please wake up **Jim and Dan**.
We will get off **the train** in another hour.

Two-word verbs are either separable or inseparable, depending on whether the object can come before or after the preposition.

Please **turn up** the sound. Please **turn** the sound **up**. (separable)

She's **looking after** the children. (inseparable)

Inseparable Two-Word Verbs

With inseparable two-word verbs, the object of the verb must come after the preposition. It cannot come between the verb and the preposition.

She's looking after **the children**. She's looking after **them**.

AVOID THE *Error*

Don't separate inseparable two-word verbs with an object.

✗ She's looking **the children** after. ✓ She's looking after **the children**.

Common inseparable two-word verbs include:

get in	get over	get through	give up
go over	keep off	look into	run into

AVOID THE *Error*

Return back is not an English construction. Use *return* or *return* + a place.

✗ We **returned back** at 2:30.
✓ We **returned** at 2:30.
✓ We **returned home** at 2:30.

Separable Two-Word Verbs

With separable two-word verbs, the object of the verb can come after the preposition or between the verb and the preposition.

He turned **the TV** off. He turned off **the TV**.

However, a pronoun can go only between the verb and the preposition. A pronoun cannot go after the preposition.

He turned **it** off.

AVOID THE *Error*

Don't put the pronoun after a separable two-word verb.

✗ Please bring back **it**.
✓ Please bring **it** back.

✗ I put away **them**.
✓ I put **them** away.

Common separable two-word verbs include:

bring back	call back	cross off	look over	talk over
look up	pick up	put away	take out	

Exercise

A *Can the underlined word move elsewhere in the sentence? Write* yes *or* no.

1. He brought up a problem.
2. She turned the lights off.
3. Let's try to get through all the exercises today.
4. I need to take the trash out.
5. I need to pick up some milk.
6. Please look over your answers carefully.
7. Please finish your test and turn it in to me.
8. We need to talk over this problem.
9. Let's finish up our work so we can go home.
10. He ran into his best friend at the mall.

VERBS
Reflexive and Reciprocal Verbs

Reflexive Verbs

We use a reflexive pronoun with a verb when the subject and the object are the same. When a verb can be used with a reflexive pronoun, we call it a reflexive verb.

He taught **himself** Mexican cooking.
She introduced **herself** to the audience.
I slipped and hurt **myself**.

The reflexive pronouns are shown in the following table:

SUBJECT PRONOUN	REFLEXIVE PRONOUN
I	myself
you	yourself, yourselves
he	himself
she	herself
we	ourselves
they	themselves

AVOID THE *Error*

The only pronouns with singular and plural forms are *yourself* and *yourselves*.

✘ John and Mary, did you hurt **yourself** on the waterslide?

✔ John and Mary, did you hurt **yourselves** on the waterslide?

We often use reflexive pronouns with verbs such as *blame*, *cut*, *enjoy*, *hurt*, *introduce*, *repeat*, and *teach*.

Mrs. O'Dowd always repeats **herself** when she's talking.
Phyllis sometimes blames **herself** for her son's problems.
It's easy to hurt **yourself** driving recklessly on a scooter.
Let's go around the room and introduce **ourselves**.

AVOID THE *Error*

Verbs such as *wash* and *shave* imply that the subject and the object are the same, but we normally do not use a reflexive pronoun with these verbs.

✘ Remember to shave **yourself** before a job interview.	✔ Remember to shave before a job interview.

In some languages, a reflexive pronoun is used with verbs such as *wash* and *shave*, along with a direct object (the part of the body being washed). In English, use only the direct object.

✘ You should wash **yourself** your hands before eating.	✔ You should wash your hands before eating.

We can use a reflexive pronoun with verbs such as *wash*, *dry*, and *shave* for emphasis.

I dried **myself** off completely before I got dressed.

Speakers sometimes use reflexive pronouns to emphasize that the subject performed the action personally.

The boss told me **himself** that we can leave work early today.
If you won't clean the kitchen **yourself**, then you shouldn't use it.

AVOID THE *Error*

Do not use a reflexive pronoun as the subject of a sentence.

✘ John and **myself** checked the shipment carefully.	✔ John and **I** checked the shipment carefully.

Reciprocal Verbs

Reciprocal verbs imply that the subjects of the verb did the action of the verb to another. With verbs like these, we can use a phrase such as *each other* or *one another*.

They met **each other** in 2007 and got married in 2008.
Those boys keep hitting **one another**.

Common reciprocal verbs include:

agree	argue	communicate	cooperate	disagree
fight	hit	meet	talk	

Exercise

A *Complete the sentences by writing the correct reflexive pronoun on the line.*

1. She fell down and hurt ________________.
2. I am going to buy ________________ a new computer this year.
3. Did you and Mark enjoy ________________ at the party?
4. John always repeats ________________ when he speaks.
5. Alan and Frank introduced ________________ to each other at the meeting.

VERBS
Infinitives, Gerunds, and Participles

Infinitives

An infinitive is the base form of the verb with *to* in front of it.

to eat	to like	to be	to take care of
to seem	to live	to run	

An infinitive can come after:

- **An action verb.** As this term implies, action verbs show action.

  I hope **to go** to China this year.
  They want him **to go** to college.
  He needs **to find** his car keys.

- **The object of a verb.** In this case, the object of the verb is similar to a "subject" of the infinitive.

  I want my kids **to go** to the circus tomorrow.
  He asked his neighbors **to be** quiet after 10:00.
  He told his son **to do** his homework.

AVOID THE *Error*

Do not use a *that* clause after *want.* Use an infinitive.

✗ I want **that you wash the dishes.**

✓ I want you **to wash the dishes**.

- **A verb such as *be*, *seems*, and so on.**

  Their usual pastime is **to watch** TV every night.
  Andrew seems **to be** tired today.
  You appear **to like** classical music.

An infinitive can be the subject of a sentence.

To know her is to love her.
To stay indoors on such a nice day would be silly.
To win is my only goal.

An infinitive and all the words that go with it are called an infinitive phrase. An infinitive can have:

- An object

The teacher wants all the students to take **their seats**.
We need to buy **some vegetables**.
My boss told me to clean **the bathroom**.

- An adverb

The librarian told the children to speak **quietly**.
She wants to leave **soon**.
I like to work a crossword puzzle **every morning**.

AVOID THE Error

In formal writing, do not split an infinitive—that is, insert another word, such as a negative word or an adverb, between *to* and the base form of the verb.

✘ I told him to **not** make so much noise.	✔ I told him **not** to make so much noise.
✘ Please help me to **quickly** wash the dishes.	✔ Please help me to wash the dishes **quickly**.

An infinitive can follow:

- *It's* + adjective

It's easy **to make** homemade bread.
It's fun **to ride** roller coasters.
It's illegal **to drive** without a seat belt.

For more information on impersonal expressions with *it's*, see page 265.

- A question word, such as *how*, *what*, or *which*

He told us how **to get** to the train station.
I don't know what **to do**.
She knows where **to buy** delicious imported Greek olives.

- A noun such as *plan*, *proposal*, or *suggestion*

  Her plan **to drive** for twenty-four hours straight seems unsafe.
  His proposal **to buy** the newspaper company surprised everyone.
  I don't like his suggestion **to have** the picnic on July 18.

An infinitive can tell the purpose of an action. You can also use *in order to* with this meaning.

She moved to Texas **to take a job**.
She went to her cottage **in order to get** away from the city for a few days.
We went to the theater **to see** *Transformers 3*.
We went to the theater **in order to see** *Transformers 3*.

Use infinitives in expressions with *too* + adjective + infinitive.

I am **too** busy **to take** a lunch break. I am going to eat at my desk.
It's **too** cold and windy **to go** to the beach. Let's go to a museum instead.
I am **too** tired **to keep** walking. Let's take a rest.

AVOID THE *Error*

Do not confuse *to* and *too*.

✗ I am **to** tired **too** watch a movie.

✓ I am **too** tired **to** watch a movie.

Use infinitives in expressions with an adjective + *enough* + infinitive.

Tanya is old **enough to vote**.
Ward is smart **enough not to buy** the first used car he sees.
You are intelligent **enough to get** into Harvard University.

AVOID THE *Error*

In everyday speech, when an infinitive follows *going*, *want*, and *got*, people shorten the verb + infinitive to *gonna*, *wanna*, and *gotta*. These short forms are OK in everyday speech, but avoid them in more formal situations and in writing.

✗ He is **gonna** arrive soon.	✓ He is **going to** arrive soon.
✗ I **wanna** buy some milk on the way home.	✓ I **want to** buy some milk on the way home.

Gotta is often short for *have got to*.

✗ I **gotta** leave soon.	✓ **I've got to** leave soon.

Infinitives Without *To*

Some verbs are followed by an infinitive without *to*. Do not use *to* after *let*, *make* (force), *feel*, *watch*, *hear*, or *see*.

The boss **let** us **leave** early yesterday.
The teacher **made** the boys **stay** after school.
I **heard** the choir **sing** a beautiful song.
I **watched** a bird **build** its nest.
The police officer **saw** a car **run** a red light.
Can you **feel** your pulse **beat?**

We can also use a gerund after *watch*, *hear*, *see*, or *feel* without a change in meaning.

I **heard** the choir **singing** a beautiful song.
I **watched** a bird **building** its nest.
The police officer **saw** a car **running** a red light.
Can you **feel** your pulse **beating**?

For information on gerunds, see page 210.

To is optional after *help*.

He helped the campers pitch their tents.	He helped the campers **to** pitch their tents.
Let's help him change that flat tire.	Let's help him **to** change that flat tire.

AVOID THE *Error*

Do not use *to* with these verbs:

- The modal verbs ***will***, ***can***, ***could***, ***may***, ***might***, ***would***, ***should***, or ***must***

✗ I can't **to** lend you five dollars. ✔ I can't lend you five dollars.

✗ I should **to** leave at six o'clock. ✔ I should leave at six o'clock.

✗ I might **to** eat a tuna sandwich for lunch. ✔ I might eat a tuna sandwich for lunch.

For information on modal verbs, see pages 174–182.

- The auxiliary verb ***do*** (***did***, ***do***, ***does***)

✗ I don't **to** like coffee. ✔ I don't like coffee.

- The verb ***let's***

✗ Let's **to** go to the supermarket after lunch. ✔ Let's go to the supermarket after lunch.

Use an infinitive with *to* with the modal verbs *ought to* and *have to/had to.*

✗ You **ought** move to a bigger house. ✔ You **ought to** move to a bigger house.

✗ They **have** finish their homework. ✔ They **have to** finish their homework.

Gerunds

A gerund is a verb + *-ing* that is used as a noun.

Swimming is great exercise.

Gerunds are spelled in the same way as present participles. For spelling rules, see page 138.

A gerund can be:

- The subject or object of a sentence

  Skiing is fun.
  I love **skiing** in winter and **playing** golf in summer.
  They started **laughing**.

As subjects, gerunds are more common than infinitives. Using an infinitive as the subject occurs mainly in writing.

To win is my only goal. (less usual)	**Winning** is my only goal. (more usual)

For more information on infinitives, see page 206.

- The complement of a verb

  Her favorite pastime is **sewing**.

- The object of a preposition

  He's interested in **learning** English.
  This pan is good for **frying** fish.
  She accused him of **stealing** her purse.

For more information on prepositions, see pages 238–255.

- The object of a verb

  I hate **ironing,** but I like **washing dishes**.

English has many expressions with *go* + gerund:

He likes to **go fishing**.
She loves to **go shopping**.
Abbie loves to **go hiking**.

AVOID THE *Error*

Not all gerunds are used as verbs, and sometimes the gerunds and related verbs have different forms.

These gerunds usually are not used as main verbs: *boating*, *rock climbing*, *canoeing*, *mountain climbing*, *skateboarding*, and *weight-lifting*. These verbs are usually used in expressions with *go* + gerund.

✗ He **boats** on weekends.	✓ He **goes boating** on weekends.
✗ Julie will **rock climb** next weekend.	✓ Julie will **go rock climbing** next weekend.

Others are used as a verb with a direct object.

✗ Steve **weight lifts** every afternoon.	✓ Steve **lifts weights** every afternoon.

A gerund can have:

- A direct object

  He is good at fixing **bikes**.

- An adverb

  She likes playing music **loudly**.

- An adjective

  The team needs **better** training.
  Mr. Smith has **poor** hearing.

We can use a name, a possessive noun, or a possessive adjective as the "subject" of a gerund.

I worry about **Victor** getting into an accident.
Chuck is upset about **her** asking for a divorce.

A gerund, its subject, its objects, and its modifiers are often called a *gerund phrase*.

AVOID THE *Error*

A gerund phrase usually does not require any special punctuation. Do not use a comma, a semicolon, or a colon to set off a gerund phrase.

✘ Getting married for the first time, is a big decision.	✔ Getting married for the first time is a big decision.

Most gerunds are uncountable nouns. However, a few are countable nouns. These are some common countable gerunds.

beginning	That movie has a boring **beginning**, but the ending is better.
drawing	He bought a **drawing** by a famous Mexican artist.
feeling	I have a funny **feeling** about that man. I don't trust him.
hearing	The prisoner will have a **hearing** before a judge on Thursday.
meeting	There is an employee **meeting** Sunday night.

painting	Here is a famous **painting** by Leonardo da Vinci.
saying	"Here today, gone tomorrow," is a common **saying**.
warning	The weatherman announced a tornado **warning** a few minutes ago.

For more information on countable and uncountable nouns, see page 51.

AVOID THE *Error*

To normally comes before an infinitive but not before a gerund. However, a few two-word verbs and other expressions with *to* can be followed by a gerund. Do not omit *to* from these expressions before a gerund: *used to*, *look forward to*, and *take to*.

✗ He is not used **getting up** early.	✓ He is not used **to getting up** early.
✗ We are looking forward **going** camping next weekend.	✓ We are looking forward **to going** camping next weekend.
✗ He never really took **working** in that factory.	✓ He never really took **to working** in that factory.

For more information on two-word verbs, see page 200.

Verbs Followed by Gerunds or Infinitives

Some verbs can be followed by a gerund, some verbs can be followed by an infinitive, and other verbs can be followed by either.

They want **to go** to the video store.
I enjoy **reading** Harry Potter books.
She loves **to dance**. She loves **dancing**.

AVOID THE *Error*

In sentences with two phrases joined by another word, always join two gerund phrases or two infinitive phrases. Do not join one of each.

✘ It's better **to have loved and lost** than never having **loved** at all.

✔ It's better **to have loved and lost** than **never to have loved** at all. (a quotation from Tennnyson, an English poet)

Verbs Followed Only by Gerunds

These verbs are followed only by gerunds:

enjoy	They enjoy **taking** long walks on the beach.
finish	He finished **watching** the movie at eleven at night.
give up	She gave up **taking** the bus after she bought a new car.
keep on	She kept on **talking** even after the teacher asked her to be quiet.
quit	She quit **smoking** last year.
suggest	I suggest **selling** that old car.

AVOID THE *Error*

Do not use an infinitive with verbs followed only by a gerund.

✘ She suggested **to order** the fish.

✔ She suggested **ordering** the fish.

Verbs Followed Only by Infinitives

These verbs are followed only by infinitives:

advise	I advised them **to be** careful.
appear	The magician appeared **to pull** a rabbit from his hat.
agree	She agreed **to meet** us for dinner.
ask	She asked **to use** the restroom.
decide	They decided **to move** to California next year.
expect	I expect **to get** paid tomorrow.

hope	I hope **to meet** her.
invite	He invited us **to go** for a hike on Saturday.
offer	She offered **to give** us directions.
plan	We plan **to leave** at 5:15.
promise	He promised **to take** his daughter to Disneyland.
refuse	Frank refused **to take** his medicine; now he's in the hospital.
remind	My mother reminded me **to take** an umbrella today.
tell	I told her **to get** ready for school.
want	My friends and I want **to go** camping this weekend.
warn	She warned him not **to leave** work early.

AVOID THE *Error*

Do not use a gerund with verbs followed only by an infinitive.

✘ He reminded her **doing** her homework. ✔ He reminded her **to do** her homework.

Verbs Followed by Gerunds and Infinitives

These verbs are followed by both gerunds and infinitives:

begin	They began **to work** at 8:30.
	They began **working** at 8:30.
can't stand	I can't stand **to hear** this music.
	I can't stand **hearing** this music.
go	He loves **to go** swimming.
	He loves **going** swimming.
hate	I hate **to wash** dishes.
	I hate **washing** dishes.
like	Anne likes **to sew**.
	Anne likes **sewing**.
love	I love **to swim**.
	I love **swimming**.
start	He started **to smoke**.
	He started **smoking**.

These verbs are followed by gerunds and infinitives without *to*:

feel	Can you feel your pulse **beat**?
	Can you feel your pulse **beating?**
hear	I heard the band **play**.
	I heard the band **playing.**

see	He saw the students **study.**
	He saw the students **studying.**
watch	I watched the boys **play** baseball.
	I watched the boys **playing** baseball.

For information on infinitives with and without *to*, see page 209.

These verbs are followed by gerunds and infinitives but with a difference in meaning:

remember	I remembered **to take** my umbrella. (I didn't forget it.)
	I remembered **taking** my umbrella. (I remembered that I took it.)
forget	He forgot **to take** his wallet. (He didn't take it.)
	He forgot **taking** his wallet. (He doesn't remember that he took it.)
try	She tried **to start** the engine. (She made an effort.)
	She tried **starting** the engine. (She experimented to see what would happen.)
stop	He stopped **smoking**. (He quit smoking.)
	He stopped **to buy** some ice cream. (He stopped the car to buy the ice cream.)

AVOID THE Error

With verbs such as *remember*, *forget*, *try*, and *stop*, use a gerund or infinitive appropriately to match your intended meaning.

✘ He forgot **taking** his wallet, so he had no money to pay for dinner.	✔ He forgot **to take** his wallet, so he had no money to pay for dinner.
✘ He stopped **to smoke** ten years ago.	✔ He stopped **smoking** ten years ago.

Participles

There are two kinds of participles: present participles and past participles.

Present participles end in *-ing*. Present participles are used with a form of the verb *be* to form the present progressive and past progressive tenses.

He is **eating** lunch.
They were **watching** TV.

For rules on spelling present participles, see page 138. For more information on the present progressive tense, see pages 136–137. For more information on the past progressive tense, see page 158.

Regular past participles end in *-ed*. There are many irregular past participles. For a list of irregular past participles, see page 164. Past participles are used with the verb *have* to form the present perfect tense.

He has **lived** here for many years.
They have **moved** to Texas.

For more information on the present perfect tense, see page 161.

Present and past participles can be used as adjectives.

Freezing temperatures are expected tonight and tomorrow.
Frozen food is very convenient.
This computer is **broken**.
I need to use a **working** computer.
This is a **fascinating** TV show.
The party was very **exciting**.

Present-participle adjectives describe the feeling produced by an object or person. Past-participle adjectives describe the feelings of a person produced by an object, person, or activity.

This class is **interesting**.	All the students are **interested** in this class.
I hate this **boring** movie.	I was **bored** during the entire movie.

Present-participle adjectives can be used in front of a noun or after a verb such as *be, feel,* and *seem*.

This is a really **boring** movie.

Past-participle adjectives can be used before a noun.

The **bored** children went outside to play.

Only a few past-participle adjectives are used after verbs such as *be, seem*, and *become*.

He seems **bored**.
She became **scared**.
We felt **pleased**.

A participial and all the words that go with it, such as adverbs or objects, are called a participial phrase. A participial phrase can modify a whole sentence. An introductory participial phrase is set off with a comma.

Getting ready for the ball, Cinderella had the help of her fairy godmother.

Bored with her homework, Linda decided to watch TV.

AVOID THE *Error*

Do not confuse an introductory participial phrase with a gerund as subject. A participial phrase requires a comma, but a gerund phrase as the subject does not.

✗ Taking a plane you will arrive much faster.	✓ Taking a plane, you will arrive much faster. (participial phrase)
✗ Taking a plane, is faster than driving.	✓ Taking a plane is faster than driving. (gerund phrase)

An introductory participial phrase needs to refer to the same person as the subject of the clause that follows it.

Driving to work, I stopped to buy a doughnut.

In this sentence, the person who was driving to work stopped to buy the doughnut.

AVOID THE *Error*

When a participial phrase doesn't refer to the subject of the main clause, it's called a "dangling participle." Dangling participles can be very confusing to readers. Fix a dangling participle by rewriting the sentence.

✗ Driving to work, **a traffic jam** slowed me down. (This sentence implies that the traffic jam was driving to work.)

✓ Driving to work, **I** was slowed down by a traffic jam.

Exercises

A *Complete the sentences by writing an infinitive on the line.*

1. I want ______________________ (**visit**) my uncle this weekend.
2. Marcella loves ______________________ (**travel**) to different countries.
3. I want Casey ______________________ (**take**) dancing lessons this year.
4. Anita and Irene agreed ______________________ (**not use**) their cell phones during meetings.
5. Gary and Elaine are too tired ______________________ (**cook**) dinner. They are going to eat in a restaurant.

B *Complete the sentences by writing a gerund on the line.*

1. ______________________ (**swim**) is a great sport.
2. Laura is good at ______________________ (**paint**) and ______________________ (**draw**).
3. Leo is interested in ______________________ (**buy**) a new car.
4. ______________________ (**eat**) too many sweets is bad for you.
5. Tim started ______________________ (**play**) the piano years ago.

C *Complete the sentences by writing an infinitive with or without* to *on the line.*

1. The coach made the players ______________________ (**run**) two miles at practice today.
2. Karen asked ______________________ (**leave**) work early so she could go to the doctor.
3. I shouldn't ______________________ (**lock**) the door. I don't have my keys with me.
4. Katie ought ______________________ (**stop**) smoking cigarettes.
5. Donna and Susan watched the team ______________________ (**play**) on TV last night.

D *Complete the sentences by writing a gerund or an infinitive on the line. If both are correct, write both.*

1. Fred and Kevin started ______________________ (**talk**) at the same time.
2. Everyone at work went out ______________________ (**eat**) dinner last night to celebrate Eileen's birthday.
3. I hate ______________________ (**iron**) clothes.
4. The bank manager advised us ______________________ (**be**) very careful with our new ATM cards.
5. We planned ______________________ (**get**) her a nice present for Mother's Day.
6. Meg and Nancy agreed ______________________ (**leave**) for the train station at 8:15.
7. I am going to stop ______________________ (**shop**) in that store. The fruit and vegetables are never fresh.
8. Leah loves ______________________ (**sleep**) late on weekends.
9. I suggest ______________________ (**try**) the onion soup. It's delicious.
10. Let's remind the mechanic ______________________ (**check**) the battery.

E *Complete the sentences by writing a present or past participle adjective on the line.*

1. I think that this movie is ______________________ (**bore**).
2. Really? I think that the movie is ______________________ (**excite**).
3. Well, I'm ______________________ (**bore**).
4. OK, let's change the channel. Maybe another show is more ______________________ (**interest**).
5. This show is about lions. Are you ______________________ (**interest**) in lions?
6. Yes, I think that lions are ______________________ (**fascinate**).

ADVERBS

Adverbs are words and phrases that modify verbs, adjectives, other adverbs, and whole sentences. Adverbs modify:

- Verbs

  He ran **quickly** and completed the race **in less than a minute**.
  She gets up **early every day**.
  They **already** finished their work.
  We stayed up **late**.

AVOID THE *Error*

An adjective, not an adverb, follows verbs such as *be*, *seem*, *become*, *feel*, *look*, *sound*, *taste*, and *smell*.

✗ This cheese smells **terribly**. ✓ This cheese smells **terrible**.

✗ You look **tiredly**. ✓ You look **tired**.

- Adjectives

  This book is **extremely** interesting.
  The meat isn't **completely** cooked.
  His hand was **slightly** hurt.
  I am afraid we are **totally** lost.

The adverbs *quite*, *really*, and *very* can be used to make many adjectives stronger.

The office is **quite** clean.
Mr. Williams is **really** nice.
That question is **very** difficult.

AVOID THE *Error*

English speakers usually do not use *very* with *delicious*. They say *really delicious*.

✗ Those cupcakes are **very** delicious.

✓ Those cupcakes are **really** delicious.

- Other adverbs

He worked **exceptionally** slowly.
She ran **extremely** fast.
Chef Smith cooks **wonderfully** well.

The adverbs *quite*, *really*, and *very* can be used to make many adverbs stronger.

He worked **really** fast and finished his work in no time.
This sports car can go **quite** fast.
Ted always listens **very** carefully.

- Entire sentences

Unexpectedly, the train left the station.
Luckily, I found my car keys in my jacket pocket.
Suddenly, some fireworks exploded in the air above us.

AVOID THE *Error*

When an adverb is first in a sentence, it's followed by a comma.

✗ **Happily** she cashed her winning lottery ticket.

✓ **Happily,** she cashed her winning lottery ticket.

Forming Adverbs

Many adverbs are formed by adding *-ly* to an adjective.

sudden	➜	sudden**ly**
slow	➜	slow**ly**

A few *-ly* words are both adjectives and adverbs.

monthly weekly daily early

My son has a **weekly** piano lesson. (adjective)
You should turn in your time card **weekly**, every Thursday. (adverb)
I am going to take the **early** bus to work today. (adjective)
I want to get to work very **early**. (adverb)

AVOID THE *Error*

Not all words that end in *-ly* are adverbs. Words such as *friendly*, *lovely*, and *silly* are all adjectives.

✗ He speaks to everyone **friendly**.

✓ He is **friendly** with everyone he speaks to.

✓ He speaks to everyone in **a friendly way**.

Spelling Rules for *-ly* Adverbs

Follow these rules for spelling *-ly* adverbs:

- Add *-ly* to most adjectives.

glad → glad**ly**
proper → proper**ly**
nice → nice**ly**
beautiful → beautiful**ly**

AVOID THE *Error*

To form the adverb form of *full*, add *-y*, not *-ly*.

✗ fullly

✓ fully

- If an adverb ends in consonant + *-le*, drop the *-e* and add *-ly*.

terrib**le** → terrib**ly**
irritab**le** → irritab**ly**
horrib**le** → horrib**ly**

- If an adjective ends in *-y*, drop the *-y* and add *-ily*.

eas**y**	➜	eas**ily**
happ**y**	➜	happ**ily**
hungr**y**	➜	hungr**ily**
angr**y**	➜	angr**ily**

- If an adjective ends in *-ic*, add *-ally*.

automat**ic**	➜	automatic**ally**
geograph**ic**	➜	geographic**ally**
histor**ic**	➜	historic**ally**
graph**ic**	➜	graphic**ally**

AVOID THE Error

The adverb form of *public* is *publicly.*

✘ public**ally** ✔ publicly

- If an adjective ends in *-ue*, drop *e* and add *-ly*.

true	➜	tru**ly**

- The adverb *good* is irregular.

good	➜	**well**

I didn't sleep **well** last night.

AVOID THE Error

Do not confuse *good* and *well. Good* is an adjective, and *well* is an adverb.

✘ My company pays workers **good**. ✔ My company pays workers **well**.

Many common adverbs do not end in *-ly*.

fast soon tomorrow hard wrong

AVOID THE *Error*

Do not add *-ly* to adverbs such as *fast* and *soon*.

✗ She ran **fastly**. ✔ She ran **fast**.

✗ The bus will arrive **soonly**. ✔ The bus will arrive **soon**.

Hard is both an adjective and an adverb. *Hardly* is not the adverb form of the adjective *hard*. These words have unrelated meanings. The adjective *hard* means "difficult":

That driving test is very **hard**.
Preparing a Thanksgiving turkey is not **hard**, but it takes a lot of time.

The adverb *hard* means "with great energy or effort."

She studied **hard** for the test.
Kelly always works **hard**.

The adverb *hardly* means "barely."

I've **hardly** lived here a year.
Conroy, you're **hardly** eating. Have some more food.

AVOID THE *Error*

Do not confuse the adverbs *hard* and *hardly*.

✗ She worked **hardly** all day. ✔ She worked **hard** all day. (She worked diligently.)

✗ He **hard** worked all day. ✔ He **hardly** worked all day. (He didn't work very much.)

Phrases can also function as adverbs.

I like to drink hot cocoa **before bed**. (prepositional phrase)
I rode the bus **for half an hour**. (prepositional phrase)
We hiked in the park **all afternoon**. (noun phrase)
My brother **hardly ever** writes me a letter. (adverb phrase)
He went to the supermarket **to buy milk**. (infinitive phrase)
They went to the party **laughing and singing**. (participial phrase)

For information on prepositional phrases, see pages 238–239.
For information on infinitive phrases, see page 207.
For information on participial phrases, see page 218.

AVOID THE *Error*

Quick and *loud* are both adjectives and adverbs. These words also have *-ly* forms. Use the *-ly* forms in more formal settings.

✗ Don't speak so **loud**. (formal)	✓ Don't speak so **loud**. (informal)
	✓ Don't speak so **loudly**. (formal or informal)

Kinds of Adverbs

Adverbs are divided into groups depending on how they modify the verb. The kinds of adverbs include adverbs of manner, time, frequency, duration, place, purpose, and probability.

Adverbs of Manner

Adverbs of manner tell how something happens. Common adverbs of manner include:

well	quickly	slowly	fast	wrong

He installed the new switch **wrong**, so now the washing machine won't start.

Let's finish our work **quickly** so we can go home before the blizzard hits.

Adverbs of Time

Adverbs of time tell when an action happens. Common adverbs of time include:

today	tomorrow	now	during March
soon	late	lately	on New Year's Eve
next year	in the fall	yet	
Monday	already	yesterday	

I need to go to the bank **today**.
Later, we went for a hike.
Victor always arrives **late**.

AVOID THE *Error*

Lately is not the adverb form of *late*. Both words are adverbs and have different meanings.

Late means "after the expected time."

✗ Victor got up **lately** every day last week.

✓ Victor got up **late** every day last week.

Lately means "recently."

✗ **Late**, I have been going swimming every morning.

✓ **Lately**, I have been going swimming every morning.

Late is also an adjective.

That teacher is very strict. She won't accept **late** work.

AVOID THE *Error*

Do not use the adverb *lately* in place of the adjective *late*.

✗ The train arrived **lately** today.

✓ The train arrived **late** today.

When days of the week are used as adverbs, *on* is optional. We can say *Monday* or *on Monday*.

He will arrive **Monday**.

He will arrive **on Monday**.

AVOID THE *Error*

Do not use the definite article *the* with days of the week.

✗ I have a dentist's appointment **the** Monday.

✓ I have a dentist's appointment Monday.

✗ We have a holiday on **the** Tuesday.

✓ We have a holiday on Tuesday.

Phrases with *ago* act as adverbs of time. These phrases tell how much time passed since an action happened.

He left **an hour ago**.
The party ended **two hours ago**.
Frank called **a minute ago**.

AVOID THE *Error*

Use the simple past tense, and not the present perfect tense, with adverbs of time that imply a completed action, such as *yesterday*, *last year*, and phrases with *ago*.

✗ He **has arrived** a week ago. ✓ He **arrived** a week ago.

For more information on the simple past tense, see page 148.
For more information on the present perfect tense, see page 161.

We often use *already* and *yet* with the present perfect tense. Use *already* in statements. Use *yet* in questions and negative statements.

Have you eaten lunch **yet**?
Yes, we've **already** eaten lunch.
No, we haven't eaten lunch **yet**.

Adverbs of Frequency

Adverbs of frequency tell how often an action happens. Some adverbs of frequency are:

always every day monthly never often

I **never** walk to work. I **usually** drive.

Adverbs of Duration

Adverbs of duration tell how long an action happens. Some adverbs of duration include:

all day forever for a week since 2007
still for two years

I have lived in Canada **since 2006**.
We camped in the state park **all week**.

Adverbs of Place

Adverbs of place tell the location of an action. Some adverbs of place include:

here there in the kitchen in out

AVOID THE *Error*

Do not confuse *there* (adverb) with *their* (possessive) or *they're* (contraction of *they are*).

✘ I went **their** after work.
✘ I went **they're** after work.

✔ I went **there** after work.

Adverbs of Purpose

Adverbs of purpose tell why an action happens. Often adverbs of purpose are prepositional phrases, infinitive phrases, and participial phrases.

I walked to work **to get some exercise.** (infinitive phrase)
I went to the park **in order to get some fresh air**. (prepositional phrase)
I went to the supermarket **for milk**. (prepositional phrase)
She walked down the street **looking for a restaurant**.

For information on infinitive phrases, see page 207.
For information on participial phrases, see page 218.
For information on prepositional phrases, see pages 238–239.

AVOID THE *Error*

Introductory infinitive, prepositional, and participial phrases are set off with commas:

✘ To get some exercise I went for a swim.

✔ To get some exercise, I went for a swim.

An introductory participial phrase should refer to the subject of the clause that follows it.

Feeling hungry, **I** headed to the kitchen.

AVOID THE *Error*

If an introductory participial phrase does not refer to the same subject as the clause that follows it, readers may feel confused. To fix this problem, rewrite the sentence.

✘ Going home, rain got in my car.	✔ While I was going home, rain got in my car.

Adverb of Probability

Adverbs of probability talk about whether an action will happen. Some adverbs of probability include:

probably possibly maybe definitely really

It will **probably** rain tonight.
Maybe we can go for a bicycle ride later.
Many children believe that Santa Claus **really** exists.

Position of Adverbs

Adverbs can be put in many different places in a sentence.

Suddenly, a car came out of nowhere and hit us.
A car **suddenly** came out of nowhere and hit us.
A car came out of nowhere and **suddenly** hit us.
A car came out of nowhere and hit us **suddenly**.

AVOID THE *Error*

In formal writing, do not split an infinitive by inserting an adverb between *to* and the base verb.

✘ I told the students to **quickly** finish.	✔ I told the students to finish **quickly**.

Adverbs of time, manner, purpose, and place are often put at the end of the sentence.

There was a terrible rainstorm **last night**. (time)
The rain fell **hard** and **fast**. (manner)
She went shopping **in order to buy a wedding present**. (purpose)
He lives **here**. (place)

When adverbs of time, manner, purpose, and place are together, they are usually in the order shown in the following table:

	MANNER	PLACE OR PURPOSE	TIME
She worked	busily	in the garden	all afternoon.
He made soup		for lunch	today.
They went		to the mall	last night.

An adverb of manner also can go before the main verb.

She **happily** (manner) planted flowers **in the flower beds** (place).

AVOID THE *Error*

Do not place an adverb of time, place, or purpose before the main verb.

✗ I **last night** read a good book. ✔ I read a good book **last night**.

An adverb of time, manner, place, or purpose can come at the beginning of a sentence for special emphasis.

Last night, there was a terrible rainstorm.
Busily, she planted flowers in the flower beds.
In the garden, there are many beautiful flowers.
In order to get some rest, he went to his cottage in the country.

AVOID THE *Error*

In formal English, people usually avoid putting *hopefully* at the beginning of a sentence. Use the verb *hope* instead. In informal English, putting *hopefully* first in a sentence is acceptable.

✗ **Hopefully**, they will win the lottery. ✔ We **hope** they will win the lottery.

Adverbs of duration usually go at the end of the sentence.

He was **in town** (place) **for a week** (duration).

Adverbs of duration often go before an adverb of time.

My mother-in-law visited us **for a month** (duration) **last year** (time).

The adverb of duration *still* goes before the main verb. *Still* can go before or after *be* as a main verb.

He **still** lives in Texas.
He **still** is a doctor.
He is **still** a doctor.

Already usually goes before the main verb or after *be* as the main verb. *Already* can go first or last in the sentence for special emphasis.

We've **already** seen this Harry Potter movie.
We've seen this Harry Potter movie **already**.
The children are **already** asleep.

Yet is usually at the end of the sentence.

We haven't finished eating **yet**.

Adverbs of frequency and probability go before the main verb. These adverbs go after *be* when it is the main verb.

We **often** have to work late.
His plane has **probably** landed by now.
I am **usually** busy.
They are **probably** lost.

AVOID THE *Error*

The adverb of probability *maybe* is usually first in a sentence.

✘ It will **maybe** rain today. ✔ **Maybe** it will rain today.

✘ It will rain today **maybe**.

Adverbs such as *very* and *really* usually go before a main verb, an adjective, or another adverb.

We are **really** going to Disneyland.
I am **very** busy.
She answered me **very** angrily.

The order of adverbs is complex, and English speakers often change the order for special emphasis. Pay attention as you listen and read to see how people change the order to emphasize different parts of the sentence.

Comparison of Adverbs

We use comparatives to talk about two things and superlatives to talk about three or more things.

Forms

ADVERBS OF ONE SYLLABLE

COMPARATIVE	SUPERLATIVE
adverb + *-er* + *than*	*the* + adverb + *-est*
faster than	the fastest
harder than	the hardest

Tim walks **faster than** Max. Harry walks **the fastest**.
Mary ran **harder than** Jane. Katie ran **the hardest**.

The comparative form of *well* is *better*. The superlative of *well* is *best*.

Lucy sings **better than** me. Ricky sings **the best**.

The comparative form of *badly* is *worse*. The superlative of *badly* is *worst*.

Barbara cooks **worse** than Laura. Hillary cooks **the worst**.

ADVERBS OF TWO SYLLABLES OR MORE

COMPARATIVE	SUPERLATIVE
more/less + adverb + *than*	*the most/least* + adverb
more quickly than	the most quickly
more beautifully than	the most beautifully
less terribly than	the least terribly

Fred finished the test **more quickly than** Anne. Irene finished **the most quickly**.
Eleanor writes **more beautifully than** Jean. Barbara writes **the most beautifully**.

AVOID THE *Error*

The comparative form of *early* is irregular. It adds *-er/-est*.

✘ I always get up **more early than** my husband.

✔ I always get up **earlier** than my husband.

Sometimes we can omit *than* from comparisons.

Work **more** carefully, please.

AVOID THE *Error*

Do not use double comparatives or superlatives.

✘ Mary swims **more better** than Anita.

✔ Mary swims **better** than Anita.

AVOID THE *Error*

You may hear *louder/loudest* and *more loudly/most loudly*. You may also hear both *quicker/quickest* and *quickly/most quickly*. Use the *-ly* versions in formal speech and writing.

✘ He ran **quicker** than Barbara and won the race. (formal)

✔ He ran **quicker** than Barbara and won the race. (informal)

✔ He ran **more quickly** than Barbara and won the race. (informal or formal)

For rules on spelling words with *-er/-est*, see pages 105–106.

AVOID THE *Error*

Do not use the comparative when the superlative is required.

✗ Barbara ran **the faster** in the class.

✓ Barbara ran **the fastest** in the class.

Do not use the superlative when the comparative is required.

✗ Between swimming and running, I like running **best**.

✓ Between swimming and running, I like running **better**.

Comparisons with *As . . . As . . .*

When the two things being compared are equal, we use *as* . . . *as* . . . .

John ran **as** quickly **as** Mary.
Michael speaks Chinese **as** well **as** a native.

Expressions with *So* + Adverb + *That*

We can use *so* + adverb + *that* to talk about actions that are extreme and their results.

She worked **so quickly that** she was finished in an hour.

AVOID THE *Error*

Do not use *so quickly as*. Use *so quickly that.*

✗ He ran **so quickly as** he finished the race in under three minutes.

✓ She ran **so quickly that** she finished the race in under three minutes.

Exercises

A *For each word, write the adverb form on the line.*

1. real ________________
2. sudden ________________
3. monthly ________________
4. fast ________________
5. slow ________________
6. easy ________________
7. full ________________
8. terrible ________________
9. good ________________
10. bad ________________

B *Rewrite each sentence using the adverb in parentheses.*

1. I'm going to leave for Texas. (**in the morning**)

   ____

2. Kathy and Rick don't get along. (**well**)

   ____

3. I can't find my wallet. It's lost. (**probably**)

   ____

4. My neighbor is going to be on a TV game show. (**really**)

   ____

5. Doris rented a DVD from the video store. (**near her house**)

   ____

6. He works downtown. (**for a large company**)

   ____

7. I stayed up last night to watch old movies. (**late**)

   ____

8. He's finished all his work. (**already**)

   ____

9. He is at work early. (**always**)

____

10. Tracy is impolite. (**never**)

____

C *Give the correct form of the adverb. Use the adverb or its comparative or superlative form. Use* than *or* the *as necessary.*

1. Mary Jane works ________________ (**hard**) Marcia.
2. My daughter got sick, so we returned home a few days ________________ (**early**) expected.
3. He drove so ________________ (**fast**) that he got a speeding ticket.
4. Of all the students in the dance class, Judy dances ________________ (**beautifully**).
5. David picked up the phone and answered as ________________ (**politely**) as possible.
6. Frank can sing ________________ (**well**) many professional singers.
7. My brother drives ________________ (**dangerously**) of everyone I know.
8. Today the team played ________________ (**badly**) yesterday.
9. Frank speaks English ________________ (**clearly**) Jillian.
10. Debbie entered the room as ________________ (**quietly**) as a mouse.

PREPOSITIONS

We use prepositions and nouns to form prepositional phrases. Prepositional phrases modify, or give information about, other parts of a sentence. Common prepositions include *in*, *on*, *at*, *until*, *since*, *for*, *before*, *after*, *during*, *under*, *behind*, *opposite*, *by*, *above*, *below*, *with*, and *about*.

The book is **on the table**.
Your appointment is **at 2:30**.
We went swimming **before breakfast**.
This book is **about the history of China**.

A noun or a gerund follows a preposition.

He is **in the office**.
On seeing the movie star, the fans began to scream.
A bus stop is **near my house**.

An infinitive can follow the prepositions *but* and *except*.

You can't park here **except to unload**.
You can't park here **but to unload**.

AVOID THE Error

An infinitive cannot follow most prepositions. Use a gerund or a related noun instead.

✘ Thanks for **to help** me.

✔ Thanks **for helping** me.

✔ Thanks for **your help.**

A pronoun can follow a preposition.

I bought this present for **you**.
I think that this book is by **him**, too.

AVOID THE *Error*

If a pronoun follows a preposition, it must be an object pronoun.

✗ Between you and **I**, she is a very nice boss.

✓ Between you and **me**, she is a very nice boss.

For more information on object pronouns, see page 88.

Prepositional phrases modify other parts of a sentence. A prepositional phrase can modify a noun, a verb, an adjective, an adverb, another prepositional phrase, or a sentence.

A woman **with bright red hair** just entered the room. (modifies the noun *woman*)
Your shift begins **at seven o'clock**. (modifies the verb *begins*)
Your shift ends at three o'clock **in the afternoon**. (modifies the phrase *three o'clock*)
I am worried **about these bills**. (modifies the adjective *worried*)
He isn't old enough **to join the army**. (modifies the adverb *enough*)
At lunch tomorrow, let's have a birthday celebration for Kate! (modifies the entire sentence)

Prepositional phrases often give information about time, location, direction, and purpose.

Time

We use the prepositions *in, on, at, for, since, from . . . to/until, until, by, before, after, during, when*, and *while* to talk about time.

In

Use *in* to talk about months, years, and seasons.

We always go on vacation **in summer**.
Taxes are due **in April**.
In 2008, the Olympics were in Beijing.

Use *in* to talk about morning, afternoon, and evening.

I always feel sleepy **in the afternoon**.

AVOID THE *Error*

Use *at*, not *in*, with *night*. Don't use *the* with *night*.

✘ like to read **in the night** before bedtime.

✔ I like to read **at night** before bedtime.

On

Use *on* to talk about specific days, such as days of the week, holidays, and dates.

I have a day off from work **on Monday**.
Your appointment is **on April 25**.
We are going to Aunt Phyllis's house **on Christmas Day** this year.

AVOID THE *Error*

Use *on*, not *in*, with the day of the week + *morning*, *afternoon*, *evening*, or *night*.

✘ I have to work **in** Friday afternoon.

✔ I have to work **on** Friday afternoon.

In general, *on* is optional with days of the week:

I have to work **Fridays** every week.

I have to work **on Fridays** every week.

We use *on time* and *on schedule* to state that someone or something is following the schedule.

The train is **on time** today.
We need to stay **on schedule**, or we won't finish our work **on time**.

AVOID THE *Error*

The opposite of *on schedule* is *off schedule* or *late*. However, the opposite of *on time* is only *late*.

✘ We are **off time**.

✔ I am afraid we are **off schedule**.

✔ We are **late**.

When we are early, we can say *early*, *ahead of time*, or *ahead of schedule*.

The train is **early**.
The train is **ahead of schedule**.
We finished **ahead of time**.

Use *on* with *weekend*.

What do you like to do **on** weekends?

Many English speakers say *over the weekend* to emphasize the amount of time.

Over the weekend, I will paint the kitchen and back stairs.

At

We use *at* to state specific times of appointments, meetings, classes, and so on.

Your appointment is **at two o'clock**.
Please meet us at the restaurant **at noon**.

AVOID THE *Error*

Do not use *to* to say the time of a meeting, appointment, and so on. Use *at*.

✘ The meeting is **to** 1:30.

✔ The meeting is **at** 1:30.

We use *it* + *be* + time to say the current or past time.

It's noon.
It **was** 8:44 when the train pulled out of the station.

For more information on saying the time, see pages 265–266.

AVOID THE *Error*

Do not use *in*, *on*, or *at* with *this*, *last*, *next*, and *every* + time.

✘	✔
I go on vacation **on** every year.	I go on vacation every year.
My husband has a day off **at** next Tuesday.	My husband has a day off next Tuesday.
The whole factory had to work overtime **in** last week.	The whole factory had to work overtime last week.

For

We use *for* to state a period of time.

We played basketball **for two hours** after work yesterday.
Mr. Jefferson has been our neighbor **for eleven years**.

Since

We use *since* to state a beginning point for an action that has continued up to the present. We often use *since* with the present perfect tense.

He's lived in Chicago **since 2000**.
That company is very old. It's been in business **since 1847**.

For more information on the present perfect tense, see page 161.

AVOID THE *Error*

Do not use *since* for a period of time. Use *for*.

✘	✔
He's had the flu **since** three days.	He's had the flu **for** three days.

From . . . to/Until

We use *from . . . to* or *until* to state a period of time.

In this part of the country, it's rainy **from** December **to** March.
Today I worked **from** 8 o'clock **until** 6 o'clock.

Until

We use *until* to state the end point of a period of time.

They stayed out dancing **until midnight**.
The shop stayed busy **until closing time**.

AVOID THE Error

In informal speech, many speakers say *till* instead of *until*. Use *until* in formal writing.

✘ He worked **till** ten o'clock. (formal writing)

✔ He worked **until** ten o'clock. (formal writing)

✔ He worked **till** ten o'clock. (informal writing)

By

We use *by* to state that an action occurs before no later than a certain time. English speakers often use *by* to state deadlines.

You must file your tax return **by April 15**.
He should arrive **by** midnight.

Before

Use *before* + noun to tell what happened prior to another activity.

Before work, I always get a cup of coffee and a doughnut.

After

We use *after* to tell an action that followed a previous action.

I went to the mall **after work**.

We can use a noun, gerund, or clause with *before* and *after*.

Before **leaving home**, I closed and locked all the windows.
Before **I left home**, I closed and locked all the windows.
He took a nap after **finishing lunch**.
He took a nap after **he finished lunch**.

AVOID THE *Error*

Do not use *that* to introduce a clause following *before* or *after*.

✘ After **that** he arrived, he checked into his hotel.

✔ After he arrived, he checked into his hotel.

During

We use *during* to say when an action happened.

During the afternoon, a blizzard struck.
The power went out **during the blizzard**.
He left work **during lunch** to go shopping.

AVOID THE *Error*

During the week means during the workweek—that is, Monday to Friday. For weekends, we say *during the weekend* or *over the weekend*.

✘ **During the week**, I relaxed on Saturday and Sunday.

✔ **During the week**, I worked overtime every day.

While

We can use *while* + gerund to talk about actions that take place during another action.

While running, she hurt her foot.
While driving to the store, I saw an accident.

While can also be used to introduce a clause.

While I was running, she hurt her foot.
While I was driving to the store, I saw an accident.

AVOID THE *Error*

Do not confuse *during* and *while.* Different words follow these words. We use *during* + noun. We use *while* + gerund or *while* + clause.

✗ We ate popcorn **while the movie.**

✔ We ate popcorn **during the movie.**

✗ We drank soda **during watching the movie.**

✔ We drank soda **while watching the movie.**

✔ We drank soda **while we were watching the movie.**

For more information on gerunds, see page 210. For more information on *while,* see page 159.

In sentences with *while* + gerund, *before* + gerund, and *after* + gerund, the gerund must refer to the same subject as the main clause.

While talking on the phone, she read her e-mail.
Before getting on the train, get your ticket punched.
After arriving, you turn your ticket in at the exit gate.

AVOID THE *Error*

If the gerund in a phrase with *while, before,* or *after* does not refer to the subject of the main clause, rewrite the sentence.

✗ While eating lunch, the phone in my office rang.

✔ While eating lunch, I was interrupted when the phone in my office rang.

Location

In

Use *in* when you think about space as an interior.

Let's go **in the train station** and buy our tickets.
It was raining, so we waited **in a bookstore** for a few minutes.

Use *in* for cities, states, and countries.

I live **in Dallas, Texas.**
People often eat dinner at ten o'clock at night **in Spain.**

On

Use *on* when you think about space as a surface.

A coffee shop is **on the corner.**
There are many beautiful houses **on my street.**
The milk is **on the kitchen table.**
Please put these books **on the bookshelf.**

AVOID THE Error

To talk about people who are riding the subway, train, or bus, we use *on*. However, we use *in* for car passengers.

✗ Right now he's **in the bus.**	✓ Right now he's **on the bus.**
✗ I think that a TV star is **on that car.**	✓ I think that a TV star is **in that car.**

On a car means "on the roof of a car."

When we talk about how we get from one place to another, we use *by*. See more information on *by* on pages 248 and 252.

We use *in* when someone is performing in a concert, play, movie, or sporting event.

I played **in a softball game** on Sunday morning.
My daughter is **in a band concert** at school on Thursday night.

At

Use *at* when you think about a space as a point.

Run! The bus is **at the bus stop.**
Stop **at the red light** or you'll get a ticket.

We always use *at* with *work*:

Usually, I am **at work** every day except Sunday.

AVOID THE *Error*

For locations on streets, we use *on* + street name or *at* + street address.

✗ Bob lives **at** Cherry Street.
✓ Bob lives **on** Cherry Street.

✗ Bob lives **on** 2121 Cherry Street.
✓ Bob lives **at** 2121 Cherry Street.

We use *at* when we state that someone is attending a concert, play, movie, or sporting event.

I was **at a baseball game** last night.
My oldest son is **at the movies** with his friends right now.

We usually use *in* and a kind of school (such as elementary school or college) to state that someone is a student. We use *at* to state that someone is currently in a school building.

My son is going to be **in high school** next year.
Right now he's **at the middle school** playing basketball.

AVOID THE *Error*

Do not use *in* + *university*. Use *in* + *college*.

✗ Tyrone is in **university** this year.
✓ Tyrone is in **college** this year.

Sometimes, we use *in* or *at* with a location to stress whether it's a public place or a building.

I have to stop **at the bank** to deposit my paycheck. (The bank is a public place.)
It's too cold **in the bank**. (The bank is a building.)

We can use *in* or *at* with *restaurant*, *coffee shop*, or *hotel*.

We ate breakfast **in** a coffee shop today. We stayed **in** a great hotel.
We ate breakfast **at** a coffee shop today. We stayed **at** a great hotel.

We use *at* to state that we are at home.

I was **at** home all day yesterday.

AVOID THE *Error*

Do not use *at* + *home,* or any preposition, when talking about traveling home.

✗ I am going **at** home right after work.

✗ I am going **to** home right after work.

✓ I am going **home** right after work.

Do not use a preposition to announce that you have arrived home.

✗ Honey, I'm **at** home.

✓ Honey, I'm home.

Behind

We use *behind* to describe something that is located at the back of another thing.

Please put these trash bags in the containers **behind the building**.
A school is **behind my house**.

By

We use *by* to describe something that is near and along the side of something else.

There is a great restaurant **by the river**.
I walked **by the store** this morning, but it was closed.

Near

We use *near* to describe something that is located close to something else.

In winter it's nice to sit **near a roaring fire**.
My house is located **near a bus stop**.

AVOID THE *Error*

Do not use *to* after *near.*

✘ His house is near **to** a supermarket.

✔ His house is near a supermarket.

Above

We use *above* to describe something that is higher than another thing.

Look! A helicopter is flying **above the football stadium.**

Over

We use *over* to describe something that is directly above something else.

A plane flew **over** the lake.
A car drove **over** the bridge.

On Top Of

We use *on top of* to describe something that is above and touching an object such as a table, cabinet, or refrigerator.

Your backpack is **on top of the cabinet.**

Often, we can use *on* interchangeably with *on top of*:

The iron is **on top of** the fridge.
The iron is **on** the fridge.

Below

We use *below* to describe something that is lower than another thing or directly under it.

From the mountaintop, we could see a beautiful valley **below us.**
The people in the apartment **below us** always make a lot of noise.

Under

We use *under* to describe something that is directly below another thing.

Never stand **under a tree** during a thunderstorm.
I always forget to vacuum **under my bed.**

We can use *below* and *under* interchangeably when they mean "directly under."

In Front Of

We use *in front of* to describe something that is directly ahead of us.

Why can't you find your car keys? They're right **in front of you**.
I found a great parking spot right **in front of the main entrance** to the mall.

AVOID THE *Error*

Do not use *in front of* to describe buildings that face one another. Use *opposite.*

✘ The bank is in front of the post office.

✔ The bank is opposite the post office.

Next To

Next to means "to one side of."

A parking lot is **next to the museum**.
The closet is **next to the front door**.

AVOID THE *Error*

Use *next to* and *by* only when the items are directly adjacent to one another. If they are not adjacent, use *near.*

✘ The bathroom is **next to** the kitchen. (They are not adjacent.)

✔ The bathroom is **near** the kitchen. (They are not adjacent.)

✔ The bathroom is **next to** the kitchen. (They are adjacent.)

Between

Between means "in the middle of two things."

The convenience store is **between the video store and the restaurant**.
Let's put a small table **between the sofa and the armchair**.

Direction

In and *Into*

We use *in* and *into* to mean "enter."

He walked **in the room** and sat down.
He walked **into the room** and sat down.
I was surprised to see a police officer run **in the store**.
I was surprised to see a police officer run **into the store**.

Out Of

We use *out of* to mean "out from inside."

The cookies are ready. Let's take them **out of the oven**.
He walked **out of the room**.

Off

We use *off* to describe movement away from the top of another thing.

The antique vase fell **off the shelf** and broke into hundreds of pieces.
Please clear your homework **off the kitchen table** so we can eat dinner.

To

We use *to* to describe movement in the direction of something.

Let's go **to the park** for a picnic.
Please open your books **to page 101**.

Toward

We use *toward* to describe movement in the general direction of something.

Let's walk **toward** the park.

AVOID THE *Error*

Do not use *toward* and *to* interchangeably. *Toward* means "in the general direction of." *To* means "directly to."

✗ I am walking **toward** her office. (I am walking directly to it.)

✓ I am walking **toward** her office. (I am walking in the general direction of her office.)

✓ I am walking **to** her office. (I am walking directly to it.)

From

We use *from* to describe movement away.

He arrived **from China** this afternoon.

We use *from* to state someone's nationality.

Carlos is **from Mexico**.

AVOID THE *Error*

To state nationality, do not use *of.* Use *from.*

✗ Eddie is **of** Mexico.

✓ Eddie is **from** Mexico.

Other Meanings

On

We use *on* to talk about TV and radio.

At work, I like to listen to music **on the radio**.
I saw a great documentary **on TV** last night.

By

We use *by* to talk about transportation.

He often comes to work **by bus**.
I am afraid to travel **by plane**.
I hate traveling **by bus**.

AVOID THE *Error*

We use *on foot* to talk about walking.

✘ He went to the supermarket **by foot.**

✔ He went to the supermarket **on foot.**

Use *by* + *bus, plane,* or *train* to talk about means of transportation.

He goes to work **by** subway. (Subway is the transportation he uses.)

Let's not drive to the art fair. Let's go **by** bus. (Bus is the transportation they will use.)

AVOID THE *Error*

Do not use *the* with *by* + *bus, train*, and so on.

✘ He goes to work by **the** bus.

✔ He goes to work by bus.

Use *on* + *the* + *bus, plane,* or *train* to talk about someone or something's location.

I forgot my purse **on** the bus.

I think that John is **on** the subway right now. He should be at work in a few minutes.

AVOID THE *Error*

Use *the* with *on* + *bus, plane,* or *train.*

✘ He's on train.

✔ He's on **the** train.

We use *by* to talk about writers or authors.

This poem is **by Shakespeare**.

His favorite songs are all **by Madonna**.

We use a prepositional phrase with *by* to state the passive subject in a passive-voice sentence.

His car was hit **by a bus**.

For more information on the passive voice, see page 191.

With and *Without*

We use *with* and *without* to talk about things we do or do not have, want, or own.

Jennifer lives **with two roommates**.
I want to buy a car **with a sunroof**.
I'd like some french fries **with my hamburger**.
I feel nervous **without my cell phone**.

About

We use *about* to talk about subjects or topics of a book, article, discussion, film, lecture, and so on.

This book is **about Abraham Lincoln**.
Let's not talk **about the accident**. It's too upsetting.

We also use *about* to mean "approximately."

It's **about two hundred miles** from here to Houston.
Right now it's **about four o'clock**.

AVOID THE *Error*

Do not use *of* to show possession. Use a possessive noun or *belongs to.*

✗ This book is **of** John.	✔ This book is **John's**.
	✔ This book **belongs to** John.

Adjective + Preposition Combinations

We use these adjectives and pronouns together.

afraid of	Tim is **afraid of** horses.
angry with	I am a bit **angry with** David.
angry about	Voters are **angry about** high taxes.

bad at	I am **bad at** math.
fascinated by	He is **fascinated by** that movie.
good at	Edward is **good at** singing.
interested in	I am **interested in** learning more about the Civil War.

AVOID THE *Error*

Do not confuse *angry with, angry at,* and *angry about.* Use *angry with* and *angry at* to talk about people whom you have a disagreement with. Use *angry about* to talk about the cause of the anger.

✘ He is angry **about** his neighbor. (He has a disagreement with the neighbor.)

✔ He is angry **at** his neighbor. (He has a disagreement with the neighbor.)

✔ He is angry **with** his neighbor. (He has a disagreement with the neighbor.)

✔ He is angry **about** his neighbor. (He is upset because of something the neighbor did.)

There are many exceptions to the rules about prepositions. As you listen to English speakers and read, take notes on the details.

Exercises

A *Complete the sentences by writing* in, on, *or* at *on the line.*

1. Please come ______________ my office and have a seat.
2. My train is ______________ 2:30 this afternoon.
3. My daughter will be ______________ college next fall. We are so proud of her!
4. When you get ______________ the bus, ask the driver if the bus goes downtown.
5. I need to buy some milk and bread ______________ the convenience store.
6. Jason is waiting for us ______________ the corner.

7. Let's meet ______________ the mall entrance ______________ two hours.
8. I live ______________ Mulberry Street.
9. I have to be ______________ work this afternoon.
10. Let's do our homework ______________ the kitchen table.
11. Let's go ______________ this store for a minute. I want to check the price of something.
12. The office is located ______________ 4250 Park Street.
13. Would you like to come to our picnic ______________ the Fourth of July?
14. ______________ China, people use chopsticks to eat.
15. I am afraid that I'm not very good ______________ sports.

B *Complete the sentences by writing the correct preposition on the line.*

about	by	by	from	in	near	off
on	over	to	with	without		

1. A plane flew ____________________ the town.
2. Kate's glass fell ____________________ the table and hit the floor.
3. I have to go ____________________ work in a few hours.
4. She always goes to school ____________________ bus.
5. To get to the waterfall, you will need to park your car and go ____________________ foot for about two miles.
6. This song was performed ____________________ Elvis Presley.
7. I have to work ____________________ 5:30 to 10:30 tonight.
8. Jean lives ____________________ her sister Mary.
9. I saw a great TV show ____________________ tornados, hurricanes, and typhoons.
10. Oh, no! I left my house ____________________ my wallet. I left it ____________________ my jacket pocket. I need to go home and get it.

C *Complete the sentences by circling the preposition.*

1. Let's sit (**near/in**) the window.
2. She is (**from/to**) Italy.
3. Everyone in the neighborhood is angry (**with/about**) noise from the new airport.
4. I'd like some ketchup (**with/without**) my french fries.

5. She lived in Chicago (**from/to**) 2006 (**from/to**) 2008. Then she moved (**from/to**) Mexico.
6. In case of fire, go (**out of/over**) the building immediately.
7. He went (**into/on**) the store.
8. I put a beautiful antique bowl (**on top of/between**) the new china cabinet.
9. They are interested (**in/of**) learning more English.
10. The drugstore is (**between/on**) the restaurant and the convenience store.

CONDITIONAL SENTENCES

We use conditional sentences to speculate about the results of actions in the present, future, and past.

If I win the lottery, I'll buy a new car. (future)
If I had time, I'd go to the movies with you. (present)
If we had arrived at the station sooner, we wouldn't have missed the train. (past)

Conditional sentences are formed with two clauses, an independent clause and a dependent clause. A clause has a complete subject and verb.

I am a teacher.
She will get a raise.

An independent clause can stand alone as a sentence.

They are my neighbors.
Dogs are great pets.

A dependent clause cannot stand alone as a sentence.

If I win the lottery
When she arrives

A dependent clause must be linked to another clause. We link dependent clauses to other clauses with words such as *if* and *when*. These words are called subordinating conjunctions.

I will always fly in first class **if** I win the lottery.

This table shows the clauses in future, present, and past conditional sentences:

DEPENDENT CLAUSE	INDEPENDENT CLAUSE
If I win the lottery,	I'll buy a new car.
If I had time,	I'd go to the movies with you.
If we had arrived at the station sooner,	we wouldn't have missed the train.

Conditional sentences have one independent clause and one dependent clause. Since the dependent clause begins with a word such as *if*, *unless*, or *when*, this clause is sometimes called the *if* clause.

If you lose your apartment keys, you'll need to call a locksmith.
We are going to go to the beach today **unless** it rains.
When the campfire is ready, we'll cook our hot dogs.

AVOID THE *Error*

Use a comma between the clauses of a conditional sentence only when the dependent (*if*) clause is first in the sentence.

✗ If I have the money I'll buy a new car next year.	✔ If I have the money, I'll buy a new car next year.
✗ I'll buy a new car next year, if I have the money.	✔ I'll buy a new car next year if I have the money.

The three types of conditional sentences are called conditional 1, conditional 2, and conditional 3.

Conditional 1 Sentences

Conditional 1 sentences talk about actions that are true or possible in the present or future.

If you are ready, we can begin the test.
If my car doesn't start, I'll call a tow truck.
If he has to work tomorrow, we won't go to the mall.

Formation

Conditional 1 sentences are formed with:

- A dependent (*if*) clause in a present tense (simple present, present progressive, and present perfect)
- An independent (main) clause in the simple present tense or future tense

If he **finishes** work early, he **will go** home.
If he'**s cooking** dinner now, he **won't want** to go out to dinner with us.
If she **has received** my e-mail, she **will come** to work early tomorrow.
If you **find** his mobile phone, **return** it to him.

For more information on the present tense, see pages 123 and 129.
For more information on the imperative, see page 142.
For more information on the future tense, see page 171.
For more information on modal verbs, see page 174.

AVOID THE *Error*

Do not use the simple future tense or *going to* in an *if* clause. Use a present tense or imperative.

✘ If I **will win** the lottery, I'll buy a new car.

✔ If I **win** the lottery, I'll buy a new car.

We can also use *going to*, an imperative, the present progressive tense, or a modal auxiliary verb in the main clause.

When we finish dinner, we **can** have some ice cream for dessert.
If you lose your driver's license, you **should** get a new one right away.
If you park near a fire hydrant, you **might** get a ticket.
If he wins the lottery, he's **going to** quit his job.
If you smell the odor of gas, **turn off** your stove and **open** a window. If the odor continues, **leave** your home immediately and **call** the gas company.

For more information on *going to*, see page 171. For more information on modal verbs, see page 174.

AVOID THE *Error*

We can also have conditional sentences with the simple present tense in the *if* clause and the simple present tense or imperative in the main clause. These sentences are often used for giving instructions or stating simple cause-and-effect relationships. These sentences are sometimes called "Conditional 0."

✘ When my car **doesn't start**, **I'll call** my husband.

✔ When my car **doesn't start**, I **call** my husband.

✘ If your phone **stops** working, **you'll check** the battery.

✔ If your phone **stops** working, **check** the battery.

Clauses with *Unless*

Unless means "if not" or "except if."

Unless it rains, we will go swimming.
They should arrive in a few minutes **unless** they are lost.

AVOID THE *Error*

Do not use *unless* when it does not mean "except if."

✘ I'd be happy **unless** we weren't going to the party.

✔ I'd be happy **if** we weren't going to the party.

Conditional 2 Sentences

We use the conditional 2 to talk about actions that are not true in the present or future tense. We form the conditional 2 with an *if* clause in the simple past tense and a main clause with *would* or *could.* Even though the verbs appear to be in the past tense, the meaning of the sentence is in the present or future tense.

If I **had** a million dollars, I **would** use the money to buy stocks and bonds.
If your car **was working**, you could pick up Joan at work.

English speakers sometimes use *were* instead of *was* in the *if* clause, especially when giving advice with, "If I were you, . . ."

If I **were** you, I'd stop smoking.

AVOID THE *Error*

Do not use *would* in an *if* clause. Use the simple past tense.

✘ I would buy a new car if I **would have** the money.

✔ I would buy a new car if I **had** the money.

Conditional 3 Sentences

We use conditional 3 sentences to talk about past actions that are contrary to fact. We often use conditional 3 to express regret about things that didn't happen.

> If I **had finished** high school, I **would have gotten** a better job.
> If she **had driven** straight home, she **wouldn't have had** an accident.

We form the conditional 3 sentence with a modal verb such as *would*, *could*, or *should* + *have* + a past participle in the main clause.

MODAL	*HAVE*	PAST PARTICIPLE
should	have	gone
would	have	written
could	have	avoided

For a complete list of past participles, see pages 164–165.

The contractions of these verb forms are *would've*, *could've*, and *should've*.

> If we had left home earlier, we **would've** arrived on time.

The contractions of the negative forms are *wouldn't have*, *couldn't have*, and *shouldn't have*.

> If you had paid attention to the traffic, you **wouldn't have** had an accident.

AVOID THE *Error*

Do not use *would of*, *could of*, or *should of* in place of *would've*, *could've*, and *should've*.

✘ If they had bought their plane tickets earlier, they **would of** got a better price.

✔ If they had bought their plane tickets earlier, they **would have** got a better price.

Do not use *wouldn't of*, *couldn't of*, or *shouldn't of* in place of *wouldn't have*, *couldn't have*, and *shouldn't have*.

✘ If I had studied harder, I **wouldn't of** received such a low grade.

✔ If I had studied harder, I **wouldn't have** received such a low grade.

Use the past perfect tense in the *if* clause. The past perfect tense is formed with the past tense of *have* (*had*) and a past participle.

PAST TENSE OF *HAD*	PAST PARTICIPLE
had	left
had	finished
had	driven

AVOID THE *Error*

In the past perfect tense, do not use the simple past-tense form of the verb in place of the past participle.

✗ If I **had went** to the supermarket, I would have bought some cheese.

✓ If I **had gone** to the supermarket, I would have bought some cheese.

The past perfect form of *have* is *had had*. Though this construction sounds unusual, it is perfectly correct.

If we **had had** a first aid kit, we could have bandaged his wound.

Nevertheless, you may want to revise your sentence to avoid the repetition.

If we **had brought** a first aid kit, we could have bandaged his wound.

AVOID THE *Error*

In independent clauses, do not use the past perfect tense in place of the simple past tense.

✗ He **had gone** to the market at 5:00.

✓ He **went** to the market at 5:00.

Exercises

A *Complete the sentences by writing the correct form of the verb on the line.*

1. If I had a million dollars, I ____________________ (**buy**) a big house.
2. If we ____________________ (**know**) that you were coming late, we would have waited for you.

3. We ______________________ (**leave**) when Victor arrives.
4. We ______________________ (**go**) inside if it starts raining.
5. I ______________________ (**visit**) my parents tomorrow if I have time.
6. If I ______________________ (**can play**) the piano, I would play happy birthday for you.
7. I would have passed the test if I ______________________ (**study**) for it.
8. If we ______________________ (**have**) more time in Disneyland, we would have gone on more rides.
9. If I ______________________ (**be**) you, I would drive more carefully.
10. Be careful! That vase will break if you ______________________ (**drop**) it.

B *Write* if *or* unless *on the line.*

1. We will go skiing tomorrow ________________ it snows.
2. I can't read the map ________________ you turn on some lights.
3. ________________ you move your car, you will get a ticket.
4. I will cook dinner ________________ you wash the dishes afterward.
5. ________________ you need a ride home, call me. I will come and get you.

C *Read the situation, then respond by writing a sentence in the conditional 1, 2, or 3, following the example.*

1. You didn't study much, so you didn't pass the test.

   If I had studied more, I would have passed the test.
2. It may be hot out today, so you might go swimming.

   ____
3. Tom doesn't have a car, so he can't give his friend a ride to work.

   ____
4. A blizzard may hit tonight. Then schools will be closed tomorrow.

   ____
5. You have the flu. You can't go to work.

   ____

IMPERSONAL EXPRESSIONS

Impersonal Expressions with *It*

A number of impersonal expressions are formed with the pronoun *it*. A pronoun is a word that replaces another noun. *I*, *me*, *you*, *he*, *him*, *her*, and *it* are all pronouns. We use the pronoun *it* as a subject or an object of a verb:

> What's that? **It**'s Tim's new car. (subject)
> I bought **it** for Mary. (object)

For more information on pronouns, see page 88.

We also use *it* in several impersonal expressions. In these expressions, *it* doesn't replace a noun.

> **It**'s 3 o'clock.
> **It**'s sunny and warm.
> **It**'s getting cooler.
> **It**'s nice to go to the beach in hot weather.

We use impersonal expressions with *it* + *be* to say the time, to describe the weather, to describe actions, and to describe commonly held beliefs.

AVOID THE *Error*

Do not confuse *it's* (contraction of *it* + *is*) with *its* (possessive form of *it*). Use *it's* in impersonal expressions with *it*.

✗ **Its** raining ✓ **It's** raining.

Saying the Time

We use *it* and a form of *be* to say the time.

> **It's** noon—time for lunch.
> What time is it? **It's** five o'clock.

We can also use *it* + *morning*, *afternoon*, or *evening*.

It's **morning**.

AVOID THE *Error*

Do not use a plural subject or verb when saying the time. Do not omit the subject.

✗ **They are** eleven o'clock. ✓ **It's** eleven o'clock.

✗ **Are** eleven o'clock.

Describing the Weather

We use *it* + *be* + adjective to describe the weather.

It's very rainy this afternoon.
It was sunny and warm at the beach.
It will be hot all afternoon.

AVOID THE *Error*

Do not use *make* to describe the weather. Use a form of *be*.

✗ It **makes** cold. ✓ It **is** cold.

We use *it* + verb to describe the weather. The verbs include *rain*, *snow*, *sleet*, *hail*, and *pour*.

It **snowed** all day yesterday.
It's **hailing** now.
It never **rains** in the Mojave desert.
It **snows** every winter in the Rocky Mountains.

We also use *it* + adjective to describe the weather. The adjectives include *sunny*, *dark*, *light*, *rainy*, *stormy*, *cloudy*, *cool*, *damp*, *hot*, *humid*, *icy*, *misty*, *muggy*, *warm*, *wet*, and *windy*.

It's **stormy** tonight.
It was **cold** yesterday.
It will be **hot and muggy** again tomorrow.

AVOID THE *Error*

Do not use *it's* + participle to describe the weather when an adjective is required.

✗ It's storming.	✓ It's stormy.
✗ It's shining.	✓ It's sunny.

We can also use other linking verbs in impersonal expressions with *it*.

It **looks** sunny.
It **seems** hazy.
It **appears** cloudy.

For more information on linking verbs, see page 121.

We use *it* and a form of *get* or *become* to describe changes to the weather.

It's getting colder and colder.
It's becoming cloudy.

Describing Actions

Expressions with *it*, a form of *be*, and an adjective are used to describe actions. A gerund or an infinitive can follow the adjective. For more information on gerunds and infinitives, see page 206.

It's easy to make chocolate chip cookies.
It's interesting living in a foreign country.
It was stupid to drive the car on the beach.

Expressing Ideas Many People Hold

Expressions with *it* and a form of *be* are used with verbs such as *believe* and *think* to express ideas that many people hold.

It's thought that nearly three million visitors come to our city each year.
It's said that Lincoln was one of the best U.S. presidents.
It's believed that Lincoln was born in 1809.

Describing Conditions

We can use *it* + adjective to describe conditions in a time or a place.

It was difficult during the Depression.

Impersonal *It* as an Object

We can use the impersonal *it* as the object of a verb such as *like, dislike,* or *hate* to describe our feelings.

I like **it** here in Taiwan.

AVOID THE *Error*

Do not omit the impersonal *it.*

✗ **Is** twelve o'clock.	✔ **It's** twelve o'clock.
✗ **Is** hard to get up early.	✔ **It's** hard to get up early.

Impersonal Expressions with *There*

There is an adverb used to describe location.

He moved to Los Angeles in 2004. He lived **there** for three years.

For more information on adverbs, see page 221.

There is also used with a form of the verb *be* in a number of impersonal expressions.

There is a spider under the table.

Describing the Existence of Something

Impersonal expressions with *there* and a form of *be* are used to describe the existence of something.

There's a nice restaurant on Main Street.
There are more than 1.3 billion people living in China.
There are many reasons for and against our proposed plan of action.
There will be a nice cup of hot chocolate waiting for you when you come back from shoveling the snow.
There was a terrible accident on the freeway last night.

In expressions with *there,* use a singular verb when the noun following the verb is singular or uncountable.

There **is** a snake under the table. (*Snake* is a singular noun.)
There **is** extra sugar in this coffee. (*Sugar* is an uncountable noun.)

For information on singular and uncountable nouns, see pages 47 and 51.

In expressions with *there,* use a plural verb when the noun following the verb is plural.

There **are** three children in the Ramos family. (*Children* is plural.)

For information on plural nouns, see page 47.

AVOID THE *Error*

When two nouns follow *there,* use a singular verb if the first noun in the series is singular or an uncountable noun.

✘ There **are** a mother duck and some baby ducklings in the pond.

✔ There **is** a mother duck and some baby ducklings in the pond. (The first noun, *mother duck*, is singular.)

✘ There **are** some flour and some chocolate chips on the kitchen table.

✔ There **is** some flour and some chocolate chips on the kitchen table. (*Some flour* is uncountable.)

When the first noun in the series is plural and the second is singular or an uncountable noun, the verb is plural.

✘ There **is** three books and a magazine on the table.

✔ There **are** three books and a magazine on the table.

We form questions with *there* by inverting *there* and *be.*

Are there more folding chairs in the storage room?
Why **is there** a clown costume on the kitchen table?

AVOID THE *Error*

Do not use *exist* in place of *there are.*

✘ **Exist** various reasons people choose to live in large cities.

✔ **There are** various reasons people choose to live in large cities.

Exercises

A *What's the weather like? Write sentences using* It's *to describe the weather as indicated in parentheses, following the example. If two answers are possible, write both.*

1. (rain) It's rainy. It's raining.
2. (sun) ______
3. (cloud) ______
4. (snow) ______
5. (wind) ______
6. (warm) ______

B *Write the time, following the example.*

1. It's 12:00

2. ______

3. ______

4. ______

5. ______________________________

C *Write sentences using the words provided and* It's, *following the example.*

1. nice/spend your vacation/beach

   It's nice to spend your vacation at the beach.

   It's nice spending your vacation at the beach.

2. interesting/read about/space travel

   ____

   ____

3. fun/watch movies/TV

   ____

   ____

4. hard/get up/5:00 in the morning

   ____

   ____

5. unusual/see snow/October

   ____

   ____

D *Complete the sentences by writing* There is *or* There are *on the line.*

1. ______________________ many reasons you should wear a seat belt while driving.
2. ______________________ a meeting in the conference room this afternoon.
3. ______________________ some rice in the kitchen.
4. ______________________ not much crime in that neighborhood.
5. ______________________ some clean towels in the closet.

E *Rewrite the sentences using* There.

1. No salt is in the food.

   There is no salt in the food.

2. A new car is in the neighbor's driveway.

   ____

3. Some doughnuts are on the kitchen counter.

   ____

4. A letter for you is on the table

   ____

5. More Christmas tree ornaments are in this box.

   ____

VOCABULARY

Reciprocal Words

English has many pairs of words with related meanings. Often, other languages use a single word for both English words.

Borrow and *Lend*

Borrow: to take from someone else for temporary use and later return

Lend: to give to someone else for temporary use and later return

Max, can you pay me the $5 you **borrowed** from me last week?
Can you **lend** me $20 until payday?

The simple past tense of *lend* is *lent.*

Bring and *Take*

Bring: to move toward a place
Take: to move away from a place

Please **bring** your books to class tomorrow.
Don't forget to **take** your umbrella with you when you leave.

Come and *Go*

Come: to move toward a place
Go: to move away from a place

Can you **come** to a party at my house on Friday?
I always **go** home from work at 5:00.

Learn and *Teach*

Learn: to acquire new knowledge or skills
Teach: to give another new knowledge or skills

I **learned** a lot in Mrs. Porter's English class. She's a great teacher.
I am **teaching** my daughter to drive.

AVOID THE *Error*

Do not confuse reciprocal verbs.

✗	✓
The bank **borrowed** him money for a new car.	The bank **lent** him money for a new car.
I didn't **come** to work today. I stayed at home in bed.	I didn't **go** to work today. I stayed at home in bed.

Confusing Word Pairs

Some English word pairs are closely related and easily confused.

Wear and *Put On*

Wear: to have clothing on your body
Put on: to place clothing on your body; to get into clothing

I am going to **wear** my new jeans to work tomorrow.
It's getting sunny. I need to **put on** a hat.

Steal and *Rob*

Steal: to take an object illegally
Rob: to take illegally from a person or institution

Someone **stole** the CD player in my car.
A criminal **robbed** North Community Bank last week.

AVOID THE *Error*

Do not confuse verbs such as *wear/put on* and *steal/rob.*

✗	✓
The bank **was stolen** last night.	The bank **was robbed** last night.
Employees should **put on** their uniforms at all times while at work.	Employees should **wear** their uniforms at all times while at work.

Make and *Do*

Make and *do* have special uses in English.

MAKE	DO
make the bed	do ironing
make breakfast, lunch, dinner	do housework
make a call	do the dishes
make plans	do the laundry
make noise	do lunch (informal)
make a mess	
make a comment	
make progress	

He **made** lunch for the guests.
She **did** the housework.
I **did** the laundry and the ironing.

AVOID THE *Error*

We say *have a party* or *give a party*, not *make a party*.

✗ I am going to **make** a party this weekend.

✓ I am going to **give** a party this weekend.

✓ I am going to **have** a party this weekend.

Language of Technology

New computer technology has given us a lot of new words:

Internet
e-mail *or* email
blog
home page
web browser *or* Web browser

There is not complete agreement on the spelling or capitalization of these words. Choose one style and use it consistently.

AVOID THE *Error*

In informal English on the Internet, users use many abbreviations to type more quickly when writing e-mails, instant messages, and blog entries. These abbreviations are OK in informal online communication, but they should be avoided in more formal writing.

✗ **BTW**, when do you get off work tomorrow?	✔ **By the way**, when do you get off work tomorrow?
✗ Please do it **ASAP**.	✔ Please do it **as soon as possible**.
✗ My name is **K80**.	✔ My name is **Katie**.

Exercises

A *Complete the sentences by writing* make *or* do *on the line.*

1. Please help me ____________________ the dishes after dinner.
2. Tomorrow I will get up early and ____________________ the laundry.
3. I hope my boyfriend ____________________ spaghetti for dinner tonight.
4. Those cars ____________________ too much noise.
5. We need to ____________________ plans for our vacation next month.

B *Complete the sentences by circling the correct word.*

1. My neighbor was (**robbed/stolen**) on the way home from work last night.
2. I want to (**learn/teach**) to ride a bike and to drive this year.
3. The bank (**lent/borrowed**) me $5,000 to buy a car.
4. Please (**bring/take**) this trash outside and put it in the trash container.
5. Last night we (**came/went**) to the movies.

CATCH THE ERRORS

Read each paragraph. Each word or phrase printed in red contains an error. Correct the errors. Check your answers in the answer key.

A My friends and me went out together on Saturday. First we had gone to see a movie on the Downtown Cinema on around 5 oclock. After seeing the movie, we went to Patricca's Pizza to have pizza. Than Mike invited my friends and I to go to his house to play pool and watching the TV. We stayed until 11 AM. I didn't want to stay late, because I wanted to go at church on the Sunday.

B My roommate and I go to the supermarket usually in the Saturday afternoons. The supermarket is more busier on the Saturday mornings, which is why we go at the afternoon. As a matter of fact we just gotten back from the supermarket a few hours ago. We bought a milk, some meats, two boxes of cereals, and a lot of fruit and vegetable. We also bought a yogurt and a biggest bottle of laundry detergent. Next, we are going to go to the laundromat to wash our cloths.

C I had a bad day yesterday. First, I had woke up late because the alarm no go off. So I putted on my clothes and run out the door. I hurryed to the bus stop, but just as I came around the corner the bus pulling away. I had to wait twenty minutes for the next one. I tryed to call my boss, but my cell phone was'nt working. Then it started rain. I hid under a tree until the bus comes. When I finally got at work, the boss yelled at me. He said, "If you will be late again, you will to be fired!" So at lunch, I buyed a new alarm clock.

D Roberts' favorite sport is rocks climbing. He practice at a gym near to his house. The gym has a high wall with some rocks in it. He wears special equipment to climbing up the wall. Last weekend, he invited me to join him in the gym. I took won look to the rock wall and said that I never should climb up. Then Robert began climb. But while he was climbing he slipped. Luckily the harness caught him, so he wasn't hurted. After that, I was really glad the wall wasn't climbed by me.

E My uncle Don is a amazing man. He has over seventy years old but he still gets up at 5:30 o'clock every day and walks for five miles. Even if it makes rain, he still walks. If the weather be very bad, he is going to an indoor swimming pool near his house. Then he swims since an hour. Then he goes to work. In weekends, he has a stand at the flea market. He sells and repairs olds bicycles. On Saturday nights he is never to tired too go dance with his girlfriend. When I am old, I hope I be like my uncle.

IRREGULAR VERB LIST

BASE	SIMPLE PAST	PAST PARTICIPLE
be	was, were	been
beat	beat	beaten
become	became	become
begin	began	begun
bend	bent	bent
bite	bit	bitten
blow	blew	blown
break	broke	broken
bring	brought	brought
build	built	built
buy	bought	bought
catch	caught	caught
choose	chose	chosen
come	came	come
cost	cost	cost
cut	cut	cut
do	did	done
draw	drew	drawn
drink	drank	drunk
drive	drove	driven
eat	ate	eaten
fall	fell	fallen
feed	fed	fed
feel	felt	felt
fight	fought	fought
find	found	found
fly	flew	flown
forget	forgot	forgotten
get	got	gotten
give	gave	given
go	went	gone
grow	grew	grown
have	had	had
hear	heard	heard

BASE	SIMPLE PAST	PAST PARTICIPLE
hide	hid	hidden
hit	hit	hit
hold	held	held
hurt	hurt	hurt
keep	kept	kept
know	knew	known
leave	left	left
lend	lent	lent
let	let	let
lose	lost	lost
make	made	made
mean	meant	meant
meet	met	met
pay	paid	paid
put	put	put
read	read /"red"	read /"red"
ride	rode	ridden
ring	rang	rung
run	ran	run
say	said	said
see	saw	seen
sell	sold	sold
send	sent	sent
show	showed	shown
shut	shut	shut
sit	sat	sat
sing	sang	sung
sleep	slept	slept
speak	spoke	spoken
spend	spent	spent
stand	stood	stood
steal	stole	stolen
swim	swam	swum
take	took	taken
tear	tore	torn
teach	taught	taught
tell	told	told
think	thought	thought
understand	understood	understood
wake up	woke up	woke up
wear	worn	worn
win	won	won
write	wrote	written

ANSWER KEY

Spelling (page 19)

1. address
2. cannot
3. their
4. misspell
5. vacuum
6. writing
7. library
8. milk
9. foreign
10. a lot

1. bears
2. nose
3. Who's
4. It's
5. Ants
6. their
7. hour
8. add
9. sweet
10. tax

1. form
2. Thank you
3. read
4. meet
5. write
6. than
7. six-pack
8. doesn't
9. opened
10. misspell

Capitalization (page 28)

1. *__I__ndiana __J__ones and the __T__emple of __D__oom*
2. **D**r. **W**illiam **A**. **W**hite
3. **M**iss **M**ary **A**pplebee
4. *__O__n the __W__aterfront*
5. **S**inclair **C**ounty **P**ublic **S**chools
6. **B**urbleson **A**ir **F**orce **B**ase
7. **A**dvanced **B**iology
8. *__V__ictory on the __H__igh __S__eas*
9. *__H__arry __P__otter and the __O__rder of the __P__hoenix*
10. **P**resident **J**ohn **F**. **K**ennedy

1. John and **I** went to **C**entury Park for a **p**icnic **l**unch.
2. Your next appointment with the **d**octor is Tuesday, **J**uly 26, at 11:30 in the **m**orning.
3. Next **s**ummer we want to go on **v**acation in **T**exas.
4. Let's go to the **m**ovies. We can see *Detectives and __R__obbers*.
5. "I **L**ove **L**ucy" is a famous TV show starring Lucille **B**all.
6. In the fall, I am going to take English **G**rammar 2.
7. I like reading **b**ooks about American **h**istory.
8. My state's **s**enator is running for **P**resident.

Punctuation (page 43)

1. ?
2. !
3. .
4. ?
5. .
6. !
7. ?
8. !
9. .
10. .

1. If I lose my job in a layoff, I will go back to school to become a medical lab technician.
2. Some cool, refreshing ice cream would taste good right about now, Anne.
3. Although the team won the first game of the play-offs, they lost the following three games and were eliminated from the championship.
4. In winter you should always wear warm clothes.
5. Ali and Fatima have several grown children, but they do not have any grandchildren. *or* Ali and Fatima have several grown children; they do not have any grandchildren.

6. I have a suggestion: let's get a new TV for the living room.
7. John likes to watch movies on TV; his brother likes to rent videos from a store.
8. Let's sell brownies, cookies, coffee cake, coffee, and tea at the bake sale next weekend.
9. He got up early, exercised, took a shower, and drove to work every day last week.
10. Sonya is very busy these days: she has a full-time job during the week and a part-time job on Saturdays.

Nouns (page 57)

1. cheeseburgers
2. sandwiches
3. parties
4. cowboys
5. wives
6. rooms
7. tomatoes
8. matches
9. oranges
10. feet
11. mice
12. boxes
13. glasses
14. zoos
15. apples
16. men
17. roofs
18. teeth
19. videos
20. lives

1. Some children
2. some milk
3. some oranges
4. some towels
5. some cheese
6. some boxes
7. some flowers
8. some bills
9. some exercise
10. some homework

C
1. box, cornflakes
2. bottles, water
3. bag, candy
4. bag, chips
5. loaves, bread
6. box, cookies

D
1. Anne's
2. women's
3. boys'
4. teachers'
5. Tony's

E
1. /z/
2. /s/
3. /z/
4. /z/
5. /z/
6. /əz/
7. /s/
8. /s/
9. /əz/
10. /z/

F
1. How many
2. How many
3. How much
4. How many
5. How much
6. Whose
7. How much
8. Whose

Numbers (page 73)

1. sixteen children
2. two thirty-five Redfield Court
3. January fifteenth, twenty-ten (*or* two thousand ten)
4. two-one-two, five-five-five, one-two-one-two
5. twenty-nine dollars and ninety-five cents (*or* twenty-nine ninety-five)
6. fourteen percent
7. one hundred one point two (*or* one hundred one and two tenths *or* one-oh-one point two)
8. seventeen and three-quarters (*or* seventeen and three-fourths)
9. twelve oh-four AM
10. six (o'clock) AM

1. Ten percent of the workers were absent yesterday.
2. Income tax is due on April 15 of each year.
3. My address is 336 Rose Avenue.
4. The total cost for your new car is $26,419.45.
5. Please be at the train station at exactly 6:16 in the morning.
6. You need $6\frac{3}{4}$ cups of flour for this bread recipe.
7. Please remember to buy 146 new books to use as graduation presents.
8. Five-thirty is very early to get up every day.
9. She won first (*or* 1st) prize in the cooking contest.
10. October 31 is the date of Halloween.

Determiners (page 86)

1. an
2. a
3. an
4. a
5. a

1. some
2. a
3. a
4. some
5. a
6. some
7. some
8. a
9. some
10. an

C

1. The
2. zero
3. zero
4. the
5. zero
6. the
7. the
8. zero
9. the
10. the

D
1. Those
2. that
3. That
4. this
5. This

Pronouns (page 98)

A
1. Please tell **her** to come to my office.
2. **They** live in this house.
3. Please put **them** in the cupboard.
4. **She** is a really nice teacher.
5. These photocopies are for **them**.
6. I opened **it** at once.
7. **We** need to work as a team to get this work done on time.
8. **He** is the manager of this office.

B
1. for
2. to
3. for
4. to
5. for

C
1. **Larry and I** are going to Las Vegas next month,
2. Everyone **is** here.
3. **She** is one of my best friends.
4. New York is a huge, busy city. **It's** a fascinating place to live.
5. Jonathan and I hurt **ourselves** at work yesterday.

Adjectives (page 109)

A
1. nice, warm, garlic
2. John's favorite, green cotton
3. dark, heavy rain
4. new, yellow, hybrid
5. expensive, antique Chinese

B
1. interesting
2. bored
3. excited
4. frightened
5. boring

1. the longest
2. deeper than
3. more expensive than
4. the best
5. the most delicious
6. more beautiful than
7. the most dangerous
8. warmer than
9. the most boring
10. higher than

Possessive Words (page 118)

1. mine
2. her
3. Their
4. theirs
5. your
6. ours
7. his
8. her
9. your
10. My

1. mine
2. your
3. our
4. his
5. yours
6. their
7. your
8. my
9. Mine
10. yours

Be: Simple Present Tense (page 127)

1. I'm
2. he's
3. she's
4. it's
5. you're
6. we're
7. they're
8. they aren't *or* they're not
9. it isn't *or* it's not
10. we aren't *or* we're not

B
1. am
2. is
3. are
4. is
5. are
6. are
7. are
8. am
9. are
10. are

C
1. isn't (*or* 's not)
2. is *or* 's
3. isn't *or* is not
4. are not *or* aren't
5. are not *or* aren't *or* 're not
6. is not, isn't, *or* 's not
7. are
8. is *or* 's
9. is *or* 's
10. are

Simple Present Tense (page 134)

A
1. lives
2. play
3. leaves
4. sends
5. checks
6. has
7. work
8. watches
9. studies
10. finishes

B
1. Where does he live?
2. When (*or* What time) do they usually eat dinner?
3. Who works in this office?
4. What does David study at night?
5. How many children does Christine have?

C
1. Mary doesn't like Italian food.
2. Frank and Mark don't drive to work together every day.
3. Maria doesn't watch TV at night after work.

4. I don't like to go to the movies on Friday nights.
5. He doesn't study English at Dyson Community College.

Present Progressive Tense (page 139)

1. Robert is cooking dinner. (*Or* Robert's)
2. Jean is setting the table. (*Or* Jean's)
3. Bob and Larry are watching TV in the living room.
4. I'm not talking on the phone. (*Or* I am not)
5. We are playing cards after dinner. (*Or* We're)
6. David is talking to a friend in Japan. (*Or* David's)
7. Vickie and Joanne are studying in the library.
8. Alan is driving home. (*Or* Alan's)
9. We are cleaning the bathrooms. (*Or* We're)
10. They are (*or* They're) taking the ten o'clock train tomorrow.

1. Are Phil and Cathy exercising in the park?
2. Is Frank playing computer games?
3. Are you listening to music?
4. Are the children playing a game?
5. Are you having fun?

1. washes
2. is washing *or* 's washing
3. plays
4. is playing
5. sleeps
6. is sleeping *or* 's sleeping
7. do
8. aren't studying, 're not studying, *or* are not studying; are working *or* 're working
9. is talking *or* 's talking
10. calls
11. make
12. are making *or* 're making

Imperatives (page 145)

1. Pass (*or* give *or* hand) me an orange, (please).
2. Don't hit your sister. *Or* Stop hitting your sister.
3. Don't speed. *Or* Don't drive so fast. *Or* Stop speeding.
4. Let's see "Transformers 3." *Or* Let's go to "Transformers 3."
5. Close the window, (please).
6. Can (*or* Could) I have the baked chicken, (please)? *Or* I'd like the baked chicken, (please).

7. Please put your shoes by the door. Can (*or* Could) you put your shoes by the door? I'd like you to put your shoes by the door.
8. Have a seat.
9. Let's check out.
10. Have a good trip.

Be: Simple Past Tense (page 147)

1. was
2. was not *or* wasn't
3. were
4. were
5. was
6. was not *or* wasn't
7. was
8. were
9. was
10. were not *or* weren't

Simple Past Tense (page 156)

1. wrote
2. called
3. didn't drive *or* did not drive; took the bus
4. used to
5. went
6. forgot
7. hit, won
8. didn't rain *or* did not rain, rained
9. told, laughed
10. didn't *or* did not cook, ate
11. had
12. slept, got
13. stayed
14. started, finished
15. had
16. did not watch *or* didn't watch, went
17. did not understand *or* didn't understand, asked
18. met
19. washed
20. tried

1. did you go
2. did it cost
3. did you cook
4. did he get up
5. didn't you go

Past Progressive Tense (page 160)

1. She was getting ready for work.
2. She was driving to work.
3. She was working.
4. She was eating lunch.
5. She was driving home.

1. was washing, broke
2. was driving, had
3. heard, were listening
4. were studying, called
5. ate, were watching

Present Perfect Tense (page 169)

1. have lived *or* 've lived
2. has left
3. Have (you) tried
4. have known
5. has worked
6. have waited *or* 've waited
7. have been *or* 've been
8. has (just) finished *or* 's (just) finished
9. Have (you) seen
10. have not arrived *or* haven't arrived
11. have lost *or* 've lost
12. has rung *or* 's rung
13. have (already) read *or* 've (already) read
14. has bought or 's bought, has not worn *or* hasn't worn
15. has had *or* 's had
16. have written *or* 've written
17. have (never) flown, 've (never) flown
18. have (you) lived
19. has not drunk, hasn't drunk
20. have found *or* 've found

1. ever; never
2. yet, yet
3. yet; already
4. since, for
5. ever, X

Future Tense with *Going to* and *Will* (page 173)

1. is going to rain *or* 's going to rain
2. am going to get up *or* 'm going to get up
3. are going to go *or* 're going to go
4. am going to do *or* 'm going to do
5. are going to eat *or* 're going to eat

1. will be *or* 'll be
2. will take *or* 'll take
3. will understand *or* 'll understand
4. will send *or* 'll send
5. will have *or* 'll have

Modal Verbs (page 182)

1. can't
2. can
3. can
4. couldn't, can
5. couldn't
6. can't
7. couldn't
8. can
9. can
10. couldn't

1. must
2. don't have to
3. had to
4. must
5. must not

1. should
2. Would
3. would
4. should
5. would
6. shouldn't

1. can
2. would
3. would like
4. must

5. should
6. Could
7. must
8. must
9. might
10. might
11. should
12. couldn't
13. shouldn't
14. Can
15. can't
16. couldn't
17. should
18. may
19. could not
20. ought

Subject-Verb Agreement (page 190)

1. is
2. is
3. lives
4. are
5. is

Passive Voice (page 198)

1. is (*or* 's)
2. is (*or* 's) being
3. has (*or* 's) been
4. was
5. was being
6. will (*or* 'll) be
7. is (*or* 's) going to be
8. can be
9. could be
10. might be

1. That song was written in 1986.
2. A great suggestion was made at the meeting.
3. This jacket was made in France.
4. Her feelings were hurt.
5. Dinner will be served at six o'clock sharp.
6. My computer has been stolen.
7. This DVD should be returned to the library in two weeks.
8. The windows weren't closed last night.

9. He is often misunderstood.
10. All the work was finished.

1. was signed
2. will be built
3. is served
4. were hurt
5. can be seen
6. has been locked
7. is being cooked
8. should be ordered
9. was offered
10. has sold

Two-Word Verbs (page 202)

1. yes
2. yes
3. no
4. yes
5. yes
6. yes
7. no
8. yes
9. yes
10. no

Reflexive and Reciprocal Verbs (page 205)

1. herself
2. myself
3. yourselves
4. himself
5. themselves

Infinitives, Gerunds, and Participles (page 219)

A

1. to visit
2. to travel
3. to take
4. not to use
5. to cook

B 1. Swimming
2. painting, drawing
3. buying
4. Eating
5. playing

C 1. run
2. to leave
3. lock
4. to stop
5. play

D 1. talking, to talk
2. to eat
3. ironing, to iron
4. to be
5. to get
6. to leave
7. shopping
8. sleeping, to sleep
9. trying
10. to check

E 1. boring
2. exciting
3. bored
4. interesting
5. interesting
6. fascinating

Adverbs (page 236)

A 1. really
2. suddenly
3. monthly
4. fast
5. slowly
6. easily
7. fully
8. terribly
9. well
10. badly

1. I'm going to leave for Texas in the morning.
2. Kathy and Rick don't get along well.
3. It's probably lost. *Or* Probably, it's lost.
4. My neighbor is really going to be on a TV game show.
5. Doris rented a DVD from the video store near her house.
6. He works for a large company downtown.
7. I stayed up late last night to watch old movies.
8. He's already finished all his work. *Or* He's finished all his work already.
9. He is always at work early.
10. Tracy is never impolite.

1. harder than
2. earlier than
3. fast
4. the most beautifully
5. politely
6. better than
7. the most dangerously
8. worse than
9. more clearly than
10. quietly

Prepositions (page 255)

1. in
2. at
3. in
4. on
5. at
6. at *or* on
7. at, in
8. on
9. at
10. on *or* at
11. in
12. at
13. on
14. In
15. at

1. over
2. off
3. to
4. by
5. on

6. by
7. from
8. with
9. on
10. without, in

1. near
2. from
3. about
4. with
5. from, to, to
6. out of
7. into
8. on top of
9. in
10. between

Conditional Sentences (page 263)

1. would buy
2. had known
3. will leave, are going to leave
4. will go, should go
5. will visit
6. could play
7. had studied
8. had had
9. were
10. drop

1. if
2. unless
3. Unless
4. if
5. If

1. If I had studied more, I would have passed the test.
2. If it's hot out, I'll go swimming.
3. If he had a car, he'd give his friend a ride to work.
4. If a blizzard hits tonight, schools will be closed tomorrow.
5. If I didn't have the flu, I could go to work.

Impersonal Expressions (page 270)

1. It's rainy. It's raining.
2. It's sunny.
3. It's cloudy.
4. It's snowy. It's snowing.
5. It's windy.
6. It's warm.

1. It's 12:00.
2. It's 3:00.
3. It's 11:30.
4. It's 5:15.
5. It's 9:10.

1. It's nice to spend your vacation at the beach. It's nice spending your vacation at the beach.
2. It's interesting to read about space travel. It's interesting reading about space travel.
3. It's fun to watch movies on TV. It's fun watching movies on TV.
4. It's hard to get up at 5:00 in the morning. It's hard getting up at 5:00 in the morning.
5. It's unusual to see snow in October. It's unusual seeing snow in October.

1. There are
2. There is
3. There is
4. There is
5. There are

1. There is no salt in the food.
2. There is a new car in the neighbor's driveway.
3. There are some doughnuts on the kitchen counter.
4. There is a letter for you on the table.
5. There are more Christmas tree ornaments in this box.

Vocabulary (page 276)

1. do
2. do
3. makes
4. make
5. make

1. robbed
2. learn
3. lent
4. take
5. went

Catch the Errors (page 277)

A My friends and I went out together on Saturday. First we went to see a movie at the Downtown Cinema at around 5 o'clock (*or* 5:00). After seeing the movie, we went to Patricca's Pizza to have pizza. Then Mike invited my friends and me to go to his house to play pool and watch TV. We stayed until 11 PM. I didn't want to stay late because I wanted to go to church on Sunday.

B My roommate and I usually go to the supermarket on Saturday afternoons. The supermarket is busier on Saturday mornings, which is why we go in the afternoon. As a matter of fact, we just got back from the supermarket a few hours ago. We bought milk, some meat, two boxes of cereal, and a lot of fruit and vegetables. We also bought some yogurt and a big bottle of laundry detergent. Next, we are going to go the laundromat to wash our clothes.

C I had a bad day yesterday. First, I woke up late because the alarm didn't go off. So I put on my clothes and ran out the door. I hurried to the bus stop, but just as I came around the corner the bus was pulling (*or* pulled) away. I had to wait twenty minutes for the next one. I tried to call my boss, but my cell phone wasn't working. Then it started to rain. I hid under a tree until the bus came. When I finally got to work, the boss yelled at me. He said, "If you are late again, you will be fired!" So at lunch, I bought a new alarm clock.

D Robert's favorite sport is rock climbing. He practices at a gym near his house. The gym has a high wall with some rocks in it. He wears special equipment to climb up the wall. Last weekend, he invited me to join him at the gym. I took one look at the rock wall and said that I never would climb up. Then Robert began climbing. But while he was climbing, he slipped. Luckily, the harness caught him, so he wasn't hurt. After that, I was really glad I didn't climb the wall.

E My uncle Don is an amazing man. He is over seventy years old, but he still gets up at 5:30 every day and walks for five miles. Even if it is raining, he still walks. If the weather is very bad, he goes to an indoor swimming pool near his house. Then he swims for an hour. Then he goes to work. On weekends, he has a stand at the flea market. He sells and repairs old bicycles. On Saturday nights he is never too tired to go dancing with his girlfriend. When I am old, I hope I am like my uncle.

INDEX OF WORDS AND EXPRESSIONS

SUBJECT INDEX